hamlyn
QuickCook

hamlyn

QuickCook

Winter
Warmers

Recipes by Jo McAuley

Every dish, three ways – you choose!
30 minutes | 20 minutes | 10 minutes

An Hachette UK Company
www.hachette.co.uk

First published in Great Britain in 2014 by Hamlyn,
a division of Octopus Publishing Group Ltd
Endeavour House, 189 Shaftesbury Avenue
London WC2H 8JY
www.octopusbooks.co.uk

Copyright © Octopus Publishing Group Ltd 2014

ISBN 978-0-600-62685-5

A CIP catalogue record for this book is available from the British Library

Printed and bound in China

10 9 8 7 6 5 4 3 2 1

Both metric and imperial measurements are given for the recipes. Use one set of
measures only, not a mixture of both.

Standard level spoon measurements are used in all recipes
1 tablespoon = 15 ml
1 teaspoon = 5 ml

Ovens should be preheated to the specified temperature. If using a fan-assisted oven,
follow the manufacturer's instructions for adjusting the time and temperature. Grills
should also be preheated.

This book includes dishes made with nuts and nut derivatives. It is advisable for
those with known allergic reactions to nuts and nut derivatives and those who may
be potentially vulnerable to these allergies, such as pregnant and nursing mothers,
invalids, the elderly, babies and children, to avoid dishes made with nuts and nut oils.

It is also prudent to check the labels of preprepared ingredients for the possible
inclusion of nut derivatives.

The Department of Health advises that eggs should not be consumed raw. This book
contains some dishes made with raw or lightly cooked eggs. It is prudent for more
vulnerable people such as pregnant and nursing mothers, invalids, the elderly, babies
and young children to avoid uncooked or lightly cooked dishes made with eggs.

Contents

Introduction

30 20 10 – Quick, Quicker, Quickest

This book offers a new and flexible approach to meal-planning for busy cooks, letting you choose the recipe option that best fits the time you have available. Inside you will find 360 dishes that will inspire and motivate you to get cooking every day of the year. All the recipes take a maximum of 30 minutes to cook. Some take as little as 20 minutes and, amazingly, many take only 10 minutes. With a bit of preparation, you can easily try out one new recipe from this book each night and slowly you will be able to build a wide and exciting portfolio of recipes to suit your needs.

How Does it Work?

Every recipe in the QuickCook series can be cooked one of three ways – a 30-minute version, a 20-minute version or a super-quick and easy 10-minute version. At the beginning of each chapter you'll find recipes listed by time. Choose a dish based on how much time you have and turn to that page.

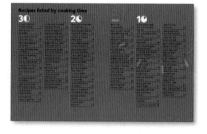

You'll find the main recipe in the middle of the page accompanied by a beautiful photograph, as well as two time-variation recipes below.

If you enjoy your chosen dish, why not go back and cook the other time-variation options at a later date? So, if you liked the 30-minute Chicken and Winter Vegetable Tray Roast, but only have 10 minutes to spare this time around, you'll find a way to cook it using cheat ingredients or clever shortcuts.

If you love the ingredients and flavours of the 10-minute Quick Pea and Leek Soup, why not try something more substantial like the 20-minute Potato, Pea and Leek Soup, or be inspired to make a more elaborate version, like Winter Potato, Pea and Leek Stew? Alternatively, browse through all 360 delicious recipes, find something that catches your eye – then cook the version that fits your time-frame.

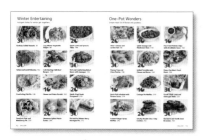

Or, for easy inspiration, turn to the gallery on pages 12–19 to get an instant overview by themes, such as Winter Entertaining or One-Pot Wonders.

QuickCook Online

To make life easier, you can use the special code on each recipe page to email yourself a recipe card for printing, or email a text-only shopping list to your phone. Go to www.hamlynquickcook.com and enter the recipe code at the bottom of each page.

WIN-FIRE-XIV

Winter Warmers

When the winter months come rolling in, often all we want to do is curl up under a warm duvet and not come out until the spring. Tempting though this option may seem, there are lots of reasons to embrace the onset of winter and the touch of Jack Frost's icy fingers. For example, it's a time to make the most of all the fantastic seasonal produce, such as the first frost-sweetened parsnips and tall, scruffy-topped leeks.

It's Cold Outside...

...so curl up by the fireside and enjoy some warming snacks and indulgent treats. Winter cooking is about getting the balance of warm spices, rich flavours, colours and textures just right, whatever the occasion. Whether you are in need of a steaming bowl of rich Spiced Tomato and Chorizo Soup (page 108), a velvet-textured Comforting Fish Pie (page 198) or even a light-up-the-senses slice of Fire and Ice Winter Berry Meringue Pie (page 272), you will find the recipe here. This is a book full of wet- and windy-day recipes created to tempt you out of hibernation, banish the winter blues and invite you into the warm, culinary pleasures of your kitchen.

Build Up Your Winter Storecupboard

As the cold winter months approach, it's a good idea to build up a stockpile of staple ingredients in the cupboard, fridge and freezer. Not only will it save trekking to the shops in bad weather, but it will enable you to whip up delicious meals at short notice.

A supply of onions, garlic, potatoes, carrots, leeks and celery is essential. If you have these, you have a great base for a quick soup or stew. And remember to keep a good array of stock cubes or, even better, homemade stock in the freezer, as these will add depth and flavour with minimum effort.

Canned food is also a great standby. Keep a selection of canned beans and pulses, such as chickpeas, butterbeans, haricot beans, kidney beans and lentils. These will bulk out a meal and also add plenty of goodness. Canned fruits and vegetables are also great for quick-fix meals, and will count towards your Five-a-day.

At a time of year when only the hardiest winter herbs can survive outside, a rack of dried herbs and spices is useful for adding flavour to everyday dishes, and can be used to create deliciously exotic and inspiring meals.

Once you have a well-stocked storecupboard, you'll only need to buy occasional extras. For example, chopped pancetta or bacon for a hearty bowl of Italian Beans with Pancetta (page 106), a chunk of fresh ginger for an exotic Quick Carrot and Coriander Tagine (page 80), or some thinly sliced sirloin for an authentic-tasting Cowboy Beef and Bean Casserole (page 110).

Where possible, it is also worth cooking dishes in bulk and freezing the extra for future use. You'll be pleased you did when you can't get to the shops and want to feed people in a hurry. Take a look through the Hearty Soups and Stews chapter (pages 72–123) for more great inspiration.

Eat Yourself to Health This Winter

Providing meals packed with nutritious, energy-boosting ingredients means that you and yours are more likely to stay fit and healthy throughout the colder months, and in this book Winter Cold-Busters (pages 124–175) is dedicated to achieving just that. It is, of course, important to eat a well-balanced diet at any time of year, but never more so than during the winter. This can be a time when your body and immune system are already weakened from lack of natural daylight and the effort of keeping warm and fighting off a variety of bugs and germs.

You can help to protect yourself from this onslaught with a combination of things. Try to take as much regular exercise as possible, ensure you are getting the right amount of sleep, drink plenty of water to stay hydrated, and eat a good and varied diet. This means consuming all the essential proteins, vitamins, fats and minerals that may seem scarce in the winter, but that are vital in the quest towards staying healthy.

The reduction in daylight hours can also take its toll and contribute to a deficiency in vitamin D, normally produced by the body when it is exposed to natural sunlight. Eating oily fish, such as mackerel, sardines and herring, can help boost your vitamin D levels and, as a bonus, contain a high level of omega-3 fatty acids, which are essential for improving metabolism.

Iron deficiency can lead to fatigue and anaemia, so it's a good idea to boost your intake by eating plenty of dark green vegetables, such as spinach and kale, red meats, oysters, mussels, lentils and chickpeas, all of which have a naturally high iron content.

If you do succumb to a cold or flu, this chapter also has recipes to get you back on your feet faster than you can say 'Jack Frost'. Why not try a soothing bowl of Feed-a-Cold Chicken Soup (page 132), an endorphin-boosting Cold-Busting Chocolate Chilli Beef (page 164), or a sinus-clearing Steamed Salmon with Chilli and Ginger (page 138)?

It is a well-known fact that, combined with regular exercise, plenty of sleep and staying hydrated, eating healthily can make a real difference to how your body and immune system cope, no matter how bad the winter weather gets. So help yourself stay on top form this and every winter, and hop over to the Winter Cold-Busters chapter for some delicious healthy-eating inspiration.

Comforting Winter Warmers

As you'll see throughout this book, comfort food doesn't necessarily have to be carbohydrate-loaded, stodgy fare, but it should have a feel-good effect and leave you satisfied. Different recipes will be comforting for different people, but, whatever your comfort food of choice, it has to suit the mood – whether that might be a wish for the simple pleasures of a deep bowlful of Pesto Spaghetti Meatballs (page 224) or the soothing comfort of Creamy Butternut and Sage Risini (page 180). Or perhaps you want to bring back fond childhood memories of Granny's Cottage Pie with Cheesy Parsnip Mash (page 218), the culinary equivalent of crawling under a warm duvet. Whatever your fancy, you will find your perfect comfort-food recipe in the Comfort-Food Main Meals chapter (pages 176–227).

Seasonal Winter Produce

It may have been said before, but it makes sense to eat foods that are in season. The wealth of fresh produce available in the supermarket all year round makes it easy to forget that certain fruits and vegetables are not actually home-grown during the winter. It's worth checking out what should be available locally and ignoring the rest. Take a look at the frozen, canned and dried alternatives, and avoid buying the so-called 'fresh' fruits and vegetables that have often travelled thousands of miles to reach your local supermarket. Instead, bring a ray of summer into your winter cooking by buying locally grown fruits and vegetables that have been frozen in season for use all year round. They will often contain more vitamins and minerals than their more-travelled counterparts, and are also easier on your budget.

Although not exhaustive, here is a list of fresh produce in season during at least some of the winter months, and for which you will find recipes in this book.

Fruit: apples, clementines, dates, figs, grapefruit, lemons, mandarins, oranges, pears and rhubarb.

Vegetables: beetroot, Brussels sprouts, cabbage, carrots, cauliflower, celeriac, celery, Jerusalem artichokes, leeks, lettuce, mushrooms, onions, parsnips, potatoes, pumpkin, radicchio, squash, sweet potatoes, watercress and winter greens.

Fish and Seafood: cod, crab, mackerel, mussels, oysters and prawns.

Put on an Apron...

...and get baking! Cheer up those long winter days by raiding the Winter Puddings, Sweet Treats and Drinks chapter (pages 228–279) and baking up a storm. What could be lovelier than coming back from a brisk, frosty afternoon walk in the countryside and having a plate of warmed, freshly baked Cinnamon-Spiked Raisin Scones (page 256) or a mountain of Chunky Double Choc-Chip Cookies (page 252) on the table in less than 20 minutes? Why not ring the changes by swapping your ordinary cup of tea for an aromatic Irish Cream Cup of Chai (page 270), and giving the children Whipped Cream Hot Chocolate (page 270), minus the alcohol, of course? The delicious aroma of home-baked goodies is guaranteed to cheer everybody up, even on the greyest of days.

Classic Winter Warmers

Comfort foods to banish the winter blues.

Garlicky Grilled Mussels 36

Lazy Winter Vegetable Hotpot 98

Quick Lamb and Spinach Tikka 148

Salmon and Lentil Fishcakes 162

Cold-Busting Chilli Beef Burgers 164

Rich and Comforting Baked Beans with Sausages 184

Comforting Fish Pie 198

Cheese and Onion Rarebit 202

Quick-Fried Steak Stroganoff 210

Freeform Pear and Blackberry Pie 254

Cinnamon-Spiked Raisin Scones 256

Fire and Ice Winter Berry Meringue Pie 272

Children Will Love These

Culinary central heating for kids.

Skier's Cheese and Lardon Tart 68

Quick Sausage and Mushroom Stew 118

Pan-Fried Polenta Chips with Arrabbiata Sauce 182

Cheesy Tuna and Chive Pasties 190

Grilled Tortellini with Cheese and Bacon 194

Deep-Pan Meat-Feast Pizza 208

Quick Fish Schnitzel with Tartare Sauce 214

Cottage Pie Waffles 218

Greek-Style Lamb and Aubergine Bake 226

Toasted Ginger Syrup Waffles 242

Chunky Double Choc-Chip Cookies 252

Mandarin and Vanilla Seed Brownies 258

Winter Entertaining

Indulgent dishes for winter get-togethers.

Onion and Mushroom
Vol-au-Vents 40

Rock Oyster Kilpatrick
with Shallots 42

Warm Fig and Prosciutto Salad
with Gorgonzola 52

Beetroot Tarte Tatin with
Goats' Cheese 60

Spicy Sardine Linguine 174

Creamy Butternut
and Sage Risini 180

Fillet Steak Bourguignon 192

Cacciatore-Style Chicken
and Salami Pasta 212

Cheat's Creamy Ham and
Ricotta Cannelloni 216

Panettone and Butter Pudding
with Raspberries 236

Brown Sugar Plum
Turnovers 244

Melting Chocolate and Date
Fondants 246

One-Pot Wonders

Simple meals full of flavour and goodness.

Quick Pea and Leek Soup 82

Peperonata-Style Pork and Chorizo Casserole 100

Italian Beans with Pancetta 106

Soupy Butternut Squash and Ham Rice Bowl 112

White Bean, Bacon and Cabbage Soup with Rosemary Pistou 114

Red Cabbage and Beetroot Tagine 158

Spiced Cabbage and Bacon Pan-Fry 166

Chestnut Mushroom and Spinach Pilau 168

Quick Fish Stew with Chickpeas 170

Wintry Fruit Salad 234

Canned Cherry and Apricot Cobbler 268

Self-Saucing Chocolate Pear Pudding 276

Hearty Meat Recipes

Satisfying feasts to warm up your menu.

30

Rosemary, Bacon and Brie
Muffins 46

20

Skier's Cheese and Lardon
Tart 68

30

Lamb and Gnocchi Hotpot 88

30

Spicy Black-Eyed Beans
and Bangers 92

20

Spiced Tomato and Chorizo
Soup 108

30

Cowboy Beef and Bean
Casserole 110

20

Mexican Beef Chilli Soup 122

10

Grilled Lamb with Kale and
Spicy Tomato Salsa 136

30

Pork, Red Pepper and
Three-Bean Goulash 154

20

Crispy Pork Milanese with
Root Vegetable Coleslaw 188

10

Spicy Sausage and
Salsa Butty 222

20

Pesto and Meatball
Tagliatelle 224

Superhealthy Fish Feasts

Omega-rich delights to boost your metabolism.

Spiced Potted Crab with Wholemeal Toasts 28

Sweet Chilli Roast Salmon Rillettes with Blinis 32

Curried Moules Marinières 48

Warm Potato and Mackerel Salad 70

Coconut Fish Laksa with Lemon Grass 94

King Prawn and Sweet Potato Curry 104

Smoked Salmon and Edamame Cups 128

Crispy Salmon Ramen 138

Poached Smoked Haddock with Fried Eggs 142

Mussel and Leek Carbonara 146

Tuna and Bulgar Wheat Bowl 152

King Prawn Soba Noodles with Sweet and Sour Dressing 156

Cheering Chicken Dishes

Protein-packed meals to tempt you out of hibernation.

1 Smoked Duck with Clementine and Walnut Salad 64

2 Chicken and Spinach Stew 78

2 Jerk Chicken and Sweet Potato Soup 90

1 Mulligatawny in a Mug 96

1 Thai Chicken Noodle Broth 116

3 Feed-a-Cold Chicken Soup 132

2 Stir-Fried Lemon Chicken with Toasted Cashews 160

2 Chicken and Brie Puff Pie 186

3 Chicken and Winter Vegetable Tray-Roast 196

3 Cajun-Spiced Turkey Meatballs 204

1 Creamy Chicken and Mushroom Rice 206

3 Feta-Stuffed Chicken with Chilli and Capers 220

Eat Your Greens

Nourishing veggie meals crammed full of good stuff.

Beetroot and Horseradish Hummus 26

Char-Grilled Aubergine and Garlic Bruschette 30

Fennel and Onion Soup with Melting Gruyère 38

Indian-Spiced Fritters with Mango Chutney 44

Leek and Chestnut Pancakes 62

Red Pepper Soup with Spicy Caraway and Chickpea Salsa 76

Quick Carrot and Coriander Tagine 80

Quick Parsnip and Lentil Dhal 86

Quick Mushroom and Garlic Tom Yum 102

Roasted Squash and Chickpea Tagine 144

Quick Spiced Cauliflower Pilau 150

Sun-Dried Tomato and Mascarpone Grilled Gnocchi 200

QuickCook

Fireside Starters, Salads and Bites

Recipes listed by cooking time

10

10 Homemade Jerusalem Artichoke Crisps with Sage Salt

Serves 4

vegetable oil, for deep-frying
400 g (13 oz) Jerusalem
  artichokes, scrubbed
2 teaspoons finely chopped sage
1 tablespoon salt, preferably
  flaky sea salt

- Heat the oil in a wide, deep-sided frying pan or saucepan to 180–190°C (350–375°F), or until a cube of bread thrown into the oil turns golden in about 1 minute.

- Slice the artichokes very thinly, using a mandoline if possible.

- Carefully drop handfuls of the sliced artichokes into the oil, and deep-fry for about 1 minute, or until the artichokes are golden. Remove with a slotted spoon and drain on kitchen paper. Repeat with the remaining artichokes.

- Combine the sage and salt. Tip the crisps into bowls and serve immediately, sprinkled with a pinch of the sage salt.

20 Warm Sage and Jerusalem Artichoke Salad

Heat 1 tablespoon olive oil with 25 g (1 oz) butter in a large frying pan and add 400 g (13 oz) scrubbed or peeled, thinly sliced Jerusalem artichokes. Cook over a medium heat, turning occasionally, for 10–12 minutes, until softened and golden. Add 1 chopped garlic clove and 2 teaspoons chopped sage to the pan for the final 2 minutes, then season with salt and pepper. Meanwhile, arrange a handful of mixed winter salad leaves on each of 4 plates. Top with the golden artichoke and sage, then scatter with shaved Parmesan cheese and drizzle with a little extra virgin olive oil. Serve immediately, accompanied by wedges of lemon, if desired.

30 Jerusalem Artichoke and Sage Pithiviers

Cook 400 g (13 oz) peeled and diced Jerusalem artichokes in a pan of lightly salted, boiling water for about 8 minutes, or until tender. Meanwhile, cook 2 trimmed and sliced leeks in a large frying pan with 25 g (1 oz) melted butter over a medium heat for 5–6 minutes, until softened. Unroll 2 x 325 g (11 oz) sheets of ready-rolled, chilled puff pastry and cut 4 x 12 cm (5 inch) circles out of each one. Place 4 of the circles on a lightly greased baking sheet. Drain the artichokes, then return to the pan and mash lightly with the cooked leek, 75 g (3 oz) Roquefort cheese and 2 teaspoons chopped sage. Spoon this mixture into the middle of the pastry circles. Brush the edges with a little beaten egg, top with the remaining pastry circles and press to seal. Brush with more beaten egg, make a small hole in the top of each one and bake in a preheated oven, 200°C (400°F), Gas Mark 6, for 15–18 minutes, until puffed up and golden. Serve hot with mixed winter salad leaves.

10 Beetroot and Horseradish Hummus

Serves 4–6

300 g (10 oz) cooked beetroot, roughly diced
2 tablespoons horseradish sauce
400 g (13 oz) chickpeas, rinsed and drained
½ teaspoon ground cumin
2 tablespoons olive oil
1 teaspoon lemon juice
salt and pepper
chopped chives, to garnish

To serve

crème fraîche (optional)
pitta breads, cut into strips

- Place all the diced beetroot in the small bowl of a food processor with the horseradish, chickpeas, cumin, olive oil, lemon juice and a generous pinch of salt and pepper. Blend until almost smooth.

- Spoon into bowls and top with a dollop of crème fraîche, if desired. Garnish with the chopped herbs and serve with strips of pitta bread.

20 Warm Beetroot Salad with Horseradish Dressing

Heat 1 tablespoon oil in a frying pan and cook 2 sliced garlic cloves over a low heat for 2 minutes, until just softened. Stir in 1 teaspoon cumin seeds and heat for a further minute, then add 500 g (1 lb) cooked beetroot, cut into wedges. Warm this for 3–4 minutes, then remove from the heat and toss briefly with 125 g (4 oz) peppery rocket leaves. Meanwhile, combine 2 teaspoons horseradish sauce with 1 teaspoon lemon juice, 3 tablespoons crème fraîche and 2 teaspoons chopped chives and season to taste. Heap the warm salad on to dishes and drizzle over the dressing to serve.

30 Beetroot Soup with Horseradish

Heat 2 tablespoons olive oil in a large saucepan and cook 2 chopped shallots, 2 chopped garlic cloves and ½ teaspoon cumin seeds over a medium heat, for 4–5 minutes, stirring occasionally, until softened. Add 750 g (1½ lb) peeled and diced beetroot. Pour 750 ml (1¼ pints) hot chicken or vegetable stock into the pan and simmer for about 20 minutes, until the beetroot is tender. Meanwhile, combine 2 teaspoons horseradish sauce with 2 tablespoons crème fraîche and 1 teaspoon lemon juice, then season to taste. Blend the soup until smooth, then ladle into bowls and serve with a dollop of horseradish cream and chopped chives or parsley to garnish.

WIN-FIRE-JYL

30 Spiced Potted Crab with Wholemeal Toasts

Serves 4

175 g (6 oz) melted butter, cooled
½ teaspoon sweet paprika
pinch of ground cayenne pepper
½ teaspoon ground mace
2 teaspoons lemon juice
2 tablespoons finely chopped
  parsley (optional)
450 g (14½ oz) crab meat
salt and pepper

To serve

wholemeal toast
lemon wedges (optional)

- Put the melted butter into a bowl with the spices, lemon juice, parsley, if using, and a pinch of salt and pepper. Beat the ingredients together.

- Add the crab meat to the spiced butter and beat again. Spoon into 4 ramekins, then cover with clingfilm and chill for at least 20 minutes, or until required.

- When ready, prepare the toast and serve with the potted crab and lemon wedges, if desired.

---

1 Lemony Spiced Crab Mayonnaise In a bowl, gently combine 450 g (14½ oz) crab meat with 4 tablespoons mayonnaise, 1 teaspoon sweet paprika, a pinch of cayenne pepper, ½ teaspoon ground mace, 2 teaspoons lemon juice and 1 tablespoon chopped parsley. Season with black pepper, mix well and serve immediately with wholemeal toast. Alternatively, chill until required.

2 Spiced Crab Cocktail with Crostini Heap 2 sliced Little Gem lettuces into 4 attractive serving bowls with a handful of watercress. Arrange 1 peeled, stoned and sliced avocado over the top with 8 quartered cherry tomatoes. Flake 300 g (10 oz) of crab meat over the salads. For the dressing, combine 4 tablespoons mayonnaise with 2 teaspoons tomato ketchup, 2 teaspoons lemon juice and the spices and seasoning from the main recipe. Cut 1 small baguette into thin slices and toast until crisp and golden. Serve the crab cocktail with the crostini and the mayonnaise dressing.

WIN-FIRE-CYB

20 Char-Grilled Aubergine and Garlic Bruschette

Serves 4

2 aubergines

2 tablespoons olive oil

4 large, thick slices of country-style bread

1 garlic clove, cut in half

150 g (5 oz) herby cream cheese, such as Boursin

4 small handfuls of watercress leaves or baby spinach

salt and pepper

chilli or extra olive oil, to drizzle (optional)

- Cut the aubergines into slices about 5 mm (¼ inch) thick and brush with the olive oil.

- Place a ridged griddle pan over a medium heat and, when hot, char-grill the aubergine slices in 3 batches for about 5–6 minutes, turning once, until softened and nicely charred.

- Meanwhile, toast the bread until golden. Lightly rub one side of the toast with the cut side of the garlic, then season lightly with salt and pepper. Spread thickly with the soft cheese.

- Arrange the aubergine over the cheese and top each slice with a small handful of watercress leaves or spinach.

- Serve drizzled with a little chilli or olive oil, if desired.

10 Char-Grilled Vegetable and Spinach Salad

Toast 2 tablespoons pine nuts in a dry frying pan for 3–4 minutes, shaking frequently, until golden. Tip on to a plate and set aside to cool. Toast 4 slices of country-style bread and spread thickly with 150 g (5 oz) herby cream cheese, such as Boursin. Arrange a handful of baby spinach on each of 4 serving plates. Combine 250 g (8 oz) shop-bought mixed char-grilled antipasti, such as aubergine, mushrooms, peppers and artichokes, and scatter over the leaves. Sprinkle with the toasted pine nuts and serve immediately with the cheesy toasts.

30 Char-Grilled Aubergine with Polenta

Place 4 chorizo cooking sausages on a small baking tray and roast in a preheated oven, 200°C (400°F), Gas Mark 6, for 10–15 minutes, or according to the packet instructions, until cooked and golden. Char-grill the aubergines following the main recipe, and keep warm. Melt 100 g (3½ oz) butter in a small saucepan over a low heat and add 2 chopped garlic cloves, ½ teaspoon chilli flakes (optional) and 1 teaspoon chopped sage leaves. Heat gently for 3–4 minutes, until the garlic is softened but not coloured. Set aside and keep warm. Bring 575 ml (18 fl oz) vegetable stock to the boil and add 100 g (3½ oz) instant polenta in a steady stream, whisking constantly to prevent lumps from forming. Cook over a low heat for about 5 minutes, until thickened. Remove from the heat and add 75 g (3 oz) herby cream cheese, such as Boursin, and beat until smooth. Season to taste. Spoon the polenta on to dishes, arrange the aubergines and chorizo sausages alongside and drizzle with the garlicky butter to serve.

Sweet Chilli Roast Salmon Rillettes with Blinis

Serves 4–6

30–36 cocktail-sized blinis

275 g (9 oz) sweet chilli roast salmon fillets (available pre-packed from supermarkets)

125 g (4 oz) cream cheese

1–2 teaspoons sweet chilli sauce, according to taste (optional)

2–3 teaspoons lemon juice, according to taste

salt and pepper

snipped chives or coriander, to garnish (optional)

- Wrap the blinis in foil and warm them in a preheated oven, 180°C (350°F), Gas Mark 4, or according to the packet instructions.

- Meanwhile, remove the skin from the salmon and flake the flesh into a bowl. Add the remaining ingredients and mash with a fork to the desired consistency. (This can be done in a food processor if you wish.) Season to taste.

- Serve the pâté with the warmed blinis, garnishing with the chives, if desired.

 Giant Smoked Salmon and Sweet Chilli Blinis Prepare the blini batter following the instructions for the 30-minute recipe. Melt a 15 g (½ oz) knob of butter in a large, nonstick pan. Using half the batter, pour 3 dollops into the pan to make 3 large blinis. Cook for 2–3 minutes, until lightly golden, then flip over and cook for a further minute. Set aside and keep warm while you make another 3 blinis. Put 125 g (4 oz) cream cheese in a small bowl with 1 tablespoon sweet chilli sauce, 1 teaspoon lemon juice, 2 teaspoons chopped coriander and a pinch of salt and pepper. Beat together, then spread thickly over the blinis. Top with thin layers of smoked salmon to serve.

 Sweet Chilli Canapé Blinis with Rillettes Sift 125 g (4 oz) self-raising flour and a pinch of salt into a bowl, then make a well in the middle. Separate 1 large egg and add the yolk to the flour with 175 ml (6 fl oz) milk, 1 tablespoon chopped chives or coriander, 1 tablespoon sweet chilli sauce, a pinch of pepper and 2 tablespoons crème fraîche. Whisk the mixture, gradually incorporating the flour from the sides, until a smooth batter forms. Whisk the egg white in a clean bowl until stiff peaks form, then fold into the batter. Place 15 g (½ oz) butter in a large, nonstick frying pan or pancake pan over a medium heat. When melted, drop small spoonfuls of the batter into the pan and cook for about 2 minutes, or until bubbles begin to form on the surface of the blinis and the underside is lightly golden. Flip over and cook the other side for 30–60 seconds, until lightly golden. Set aside and keep warm while you make about 30 more blinis in the same way, adding extra butter each time if necessary. Meanwhile, prepare the salmon rillettes following the main recipe. Serve the canapé blinis with the prepared rillettes.

Warm Mushroom Salad Crostini

Serves 4

75 g (3 oz) butter
2 garlic cloves, chopped
1 tablespoon chopped herbs,
   such as chervil, parsley,
   tarragon and chives
250 g (8 oz) mixed mushrooms,
   such as portobello, ceps, porcini,
   girolle, thickly sliced
sourdough or country-style
   bread, thinly sliced

- Melt the butter in a large frying pan with the garlic and herbs until just beginning to foam. Add the mushrooms and fry over a medium heat for 4–5 minutes, until soft and golden.

- Meanwhile, heat a ridged griddle pan. When hot, toast the bread in it until golden and nicely charred. To serve, arrange the crostini on plates and spoon over the buttery mushrooms.

Creamy Baked Egg and Mushroom

Pots Fry the mushrooms following the main recipe. Meanwhile, mix 150 ml (¼ pint) double cream in a bowl with a pinch of salt and pepper. Stir the mushrooms into the cream, then divide between 4 ovenproof ramekins. Crack an egg into each ramekin and place the dishes in a roasting tin. Half-fill the tin with hot water, then place in a preheated oven, 200°C (400°F), Gas Mark 6, for 7–8 minutes, until the eggs are set but the yolk is still slightly runny. Remove from the oven and serve immediately with toasted sourdough.

Roast Field Mushrooms in

Red Wine Place 12 small field or portobellini mushrooms in a bowl and toss with 3 tablespoons olive oil, 125 ml (4 fl oz) full-bodied red wine, 2 chopped garlic cloves, 2 tablespoons chopped parsley and a generous pinch of salt and pepper. Arrange stalk-side up in a snug-fitting, ovenproof dish and roast in a preheated oven, 190°C (375°F), Gas Mark 5, for about 15 minutes, until softened. Serve over toasted sourdough with the warm juices and plenty of extra chopped parsley.

30 Garlicky Grilled Mussels

Serves 4

50 g (2 oz) butter
2 shallots, chopped
3 garlic cloves, chopped
125 ml (4 fl oz) dry white wine
625 g (1¼ lb) mussels, debearded
  and scrubbed
50 g (2 oz) coarse breadcrumbs
2 tablespoons finely chopped
  parsley
1 teaspoon finely grated
  lemon rind
2 tablespoons freshly grated
  Parmesan cheese
1 tablespoon olive oil

- Melt the butter in a large saucepan over a medium-low heat and cook the shallots and 2 of the garlic cloves for 5–6 minutes, until softened. Pour in the wine, increase the heat slightly and bring to the boil.

- Tip the mussels into the pan, discarding any that won't close when sharply tapped, then cover and simmer gently for 3–5 minutes, shaking the pan occasionally, until the shells are opened. Discard any that remain closed. Set aside until cool enough to handle.

- Meanwhile, put the breadcrumbs in a bowl with the parsley, remaining garlic, lemon rind, Parmesan and oil and mix well.

- Discard the empty half-shell from each mussel and arrange the mussels in a single layer on a large baking sheet.

- Spoon the breadcrumb mixture neatly over the mussels and slide under a preheated, medium grill, for 2–3 minutes, or until the breadcrumbs are crisp and golden.

---

1 0 Mussels in Garlic Butter Sauce

Melt 50 g (2 oz) butter in a frying pan with 2 chopped shallots and 3 chopped garlic cloves. Cook over a low heat for 2–3 minutes, then add 75 ml (3 fl oz) dry white wine and 2 teaspoons Pernod (optional). Simmer for 3–4 minutes. Tip 400 g (13 oz) cooked, shelled mussels into the pan and reheat quickly. Take off the heat and stir in 2 tablespoons double cream. Season, scatter over 2 tablespoons chopped parsley and spoon into shallow dishes. Serve immediately.

2 0 Herby Garlic Butter Mussel

Parcels Melt 50 g (2 oz) butter in a frying pan with 2 chopped garlic cloves for 2–3 minutes, until softened. Add 2 tablespoons chopped parsley, 1 teaspoon Pernod (optional) and 250 g (8 oz) cooked, shelled mussels. Stir for 1 minute, then remove from the heat. Brush 4 large sheets of filo pastry with melted butter, then fold in half. Spoon the mussels on to one end of each pastry strip, then fold up to form brick-shaped parcels, tucking in the edges as you fold.

Melt 25 g (1 oz) butter in a clean frying pan with 1 tablespoon olive oil and cook the parcels for about 8–10 minutes, turning occasionally, until crisp and golden. Serve with salad leaves and French bread.

3⦿ Fennel and Onion Soup with Melting Gruyère

Serves 4

75 g (3 oz) butter
1 head of fennel, thinly sliced
2 large onions, halved and
thinly sliced
2 garlic cloves, roughly chopped
2 teaspoons chopped thyme
1 teaspoon dark soft brown sugar
3 tablespoons brandy or dry sherry
750 ml (1¼ pints) hot beef stock
1 teaspoon dark soy sauce
(optional)
4 small slices of sourdough bread
100 g (3½ oz) finely grated
Gruyère or Emmental cheese
salt and pepper

- Melt the butter in a large saucepan over a medium-low heat and cook the fennel, onions, garlic, thyme and sugar for about 20 minutes, stirring occasionally, until soft and slightly caramelized.

- Pour in the brandy or sherry and heat until completely evaporated. Add the stock and soy sauce, if using, and bring to the boil, then simmer gently for about 5 minutes. Season to taste.

- Meanwhile, top the slices of sourdough with the grated cheese and arrange on a foil-lined grill rack. Place under a preheated medium-hot grill for 2–3 minutes, until the cheese is melting.

- To serve, ladle the soup into bowls and top with the Gruyère toasts.

 Quick Fennel and Gruyère Salad
Slice 1 trimmed head of fennel very thinly, using a mandoline if possible. Place in a bowl with 1 thinly sliced celery stick, 1 thinly sliced red onion, 1 peeled, cored and thinly sliced dessert apple and 100 g (3½ oz) mixed salad leaves. Drizzle over 2 tablespoons olive oil and 2 teaspoons lemon juice. Season with salt and pepper, then toss lightly to coat. Heap on to serving plates and top with 50 g (2 oz) shaved Gruyère and 1 teaspoon roughly chopped fennel fronds or dill. Serve the salad immediately.

 Pan-Fried Fennel and Onion Salad with Gruyère Toasts Cut 1 head of trimmed fennel into thin wedges. Melt 50 g (2 oz) butter in a large frying pan and fry the fennel and 1 sliced red onion over a medium heat for about 10 minutes, turning occasionally, until slightly softened and golden. Stir in 1 teaspoon fennel seeds, 1 teaspoon chopped thyme and a sprinkling of salt and pepper. Pour in 2 tablespoons Pernod or pastis and simmer until completely evaporated. Take off the heat and toss briefly with 2 handfuls frisée-style salad leaves. Heap on to plates and serve topped with the Gruyère toasts from the main recipe.

Onion and Mushroom Vol-au-Vents

Makes 16

16 frozen vol-au-vent cases
50 g (2 oz) butter
1 small onion, finely chopped
1 garlic clove, chopped
250 g (8 oz) mixed mushrooms, thinly sliced
125 g (4 oz) mascarpone cheese
2 teaspoons chopped herbs, such as tarragon, chervil and chives, plus extra to garnish (optional)
salt and pepper

- Line a baking sheet with baking paper. Arrange the vol-au-vent cases on it and bake in a preheated oven, 220°C (425°F), Gas Mark 7, for 10–12 minutes, or according to the packet instructions, until crisp and golden.

- Meanwhile, melt the butter in a frying pan and cook the onion and garlic over a medium heat for 6–7 minutes, stirring occasionally, until softened and golden. Add the mushrooms and fry for a further 3–4 minutes, until softened.

- Stir the mascarpone and herbs into the pan, add a pinch of salt and pepper, then remove from the heat.

- Spoon the filling into the pastry cases and serve warm, garnished with freshly snipped chives, if desired.

Onion and Mushroom Focaccia

Very thinly slice 150 g (5 oz) chestnut mushrooms and scatter over a focaccia or similar flat loaf. Top with half a very thinly sliced red onion, drizzle with 1 tablespoon olive oil and sprinkle over ½ teaspoon dried thyme. Place in a preheated oven, 200°C (400°F), Gas Mark 6, for 6–7 minutes, until hot and lightly coloured. Cut into fingers to serve.

Onion and Mushroom Tart

Cut a 1.5 cm (¾ inch) border around the edge of a 375 g (12 oz) sheet of ready-rolled, chilled puff pastry and place on a baking sheet lined with baking paper. Mix 1 tablespoon chopped chives, 2 tablespoons caramelized onions and a pinch of salt and pepper into 3 tablespoons mascarpone. Spread evenly over the pastry, keeping within the border.

Scatter 150 g (5 oz) thinly sliced mushrooms and half a thinly sliced red onion over the top, and sprinkle with 2 tablespoons freshly grated Parmesan cheese. Bake in a preheated oven, 200°C (400°F), Gas Mark 6, for about 15–20 minutes, until crisp and golden. Serve with plenty of green salad.

Rock Oyster Kilpatrick with Shallots

Serves 4

coarse sea salt

16 large rock oysters

1 tablespoon olive oil

4 rindless streaky bacon rashers, finely chopped

2 banana shallots, finely chopped

2 tablespoons flat leaf parsley, chopped

2 teaspoons Worcestershire sauce

few drops of Tabasco sauce (optional)

50 g (2 oz) slightly stale breadcrumbs

lemon wedges, to serve (optional)

- Cover a baking sheet with a thick layer of coarse sea salt.

- Wrap one hand in a tea towel and hold an oyster in it flat-side up with the 'hinge' pointing towards you. Insert the tip of an oyster knife into the hinge, force it into the gap, then twist the knife until the shell opens. Push the knife in deeper and run it along the top of the shell to cut through the muscle that attaches the oyster to it. Discard the top shell. Remove any grit from the oyster, taking care not to lose any of the liquid inside the shell. Run the knife underneath the oyster to cut through the muscle attached to the bottom shell. Place the open oyster on the baking sheet and repeat this process with the remaining oysters.

- Heat the oil in a frying pan and fry the bacon for 6–7 minutes, stirring occasionally. Drain on kitchen paper. Fry the shallots in the bacon fat over a medium-low heat for 4–5 minutes. Tip into a bowl, add the bacon, parsley and Worcestershire sauce, and Tabasco, if desired. Mix well.

- Return the pan to the heat and add the breadcrumbs, with a little more oil if necessary. Stir-fry for 4–5 minutes. Add to the bacon mixture and stir well. Spoon the topping over the oysters, then slide under a preheated, medium-hot grill for 1–2 minutes. Serve immediately with lemon wedges, if desired.

 Rock Oysters with Shallot Vinegar

Chop 2 shallots and mix with 3 tablespoons red wine vinegar and a pinch of salt and sugar. Open 12–16 oysters, as above, and arrange on 4 serving plates, using a bed of rock salt to keep them upright if you wish. Serve with a small dish of shallot vinegar and Tabasco sauce.

Simple Grilled Oysters with Shallots Open 12–16 oysters, as in the main recipe. Arrange them on a baking sheet covered with rock salt. Scatter 2 finely chopped slices of Parma ham over the oysters, followed by 2 finely chopped shallots. Top each one with a drop of Worcestershire sauce and slide under a preheated, medium-hot grill for 1–2 minutes. Transfer to serving plates and serve immediately with a few drops of Tabasco sauce, if desired.

20 Indian-Spiced Fritters with Mango Chutney

Serves 4

2 eggs
500 g (1 lb) sweet potatoes, coarsely grated
1 onion, thinly sliced
2 teaspoons peeled and freshly grated root ginger
150 g (5 oz) flour
1 teaspoon cumin seeds
1 teaspoon ground coriander
½ teaspoon ground turmeric (optional)
¼ teaspoon cayenne pepper
3 tablespoons vegetable oil
salt and pepper
coriander leaves, to garnish
mango chutney, to serve

- Beat the eggs in a bowl. Add the sweet potatoes, onion and ginger and mix well. Sprinkle over the flour, spices and seasoning and mix really well.

- Heat the oil in a large frying pan and place large spoonfuls of the mixture in the pan, flattening slightly with the back of a spatula. Cook for 5–6 minutes over a medium heat, turning once, until crisp and golden. Drain on kitchen paper and keep warm. Repeat with remaining mixture.

- Arrange the fritters on plates, garnish with coriander leaves and serve with mango chutney.

 Poppadums with Indian Spices and Mango Chutney Heat 3.5 cm (1½ inches) vegetable oil in a deep-sided frying pan to 180–190°C (350–375°F), or until a cube of bread browns in 1 minute. Deep-fry 8 poppadums, one at a time, for 30–45 seconds, or according to the packet instructions, until puffed and crisp. Drain on kitchen paper. Combine ½ teaspoon each of ground cumin and coriander with a pinch of hot chilli powder and ¼ teaspoon ground turmeric. Dust the poppadums in the spice mix and serve with mango chutney and Indian pickles.

 Indian-Spiced Scones with Mango Chutney Place 200 g (7 oz) self-raising flour in a bowl, add 1 teaspoon baking powder, 1 teaspoon salt, 1 teaspoon each of ground cumin and coriander, ½ teaspoon ground turmeric and ¼ teaspoon hot chilli powder. Mix well. Add 75 g (3 oz) diced butter and rub in with the fingertips until the mixture resembles fine breadcrumbs. Add half a finely chopped red onion, 2 tablespoons chopped coriander, 2 tablespoons mango chutney, 1 large beaten egg and 3–4 tablespoons of milk – just enough to form a soft dough. Turn the dough on to a lightly floured work surface and roll out to a thickness of 1.5 cm (¾ inch). Using a 6 cm (2½ inch) cutter, stamp out 8 circles. Place on a baking sheet lined with baking paper and bake in a preheated oven, 220°C (425°F), Gas Mark 7, for about 15 minutes, until risen and golden. Transfer to a wire rack to cool slightly, then serve warm with a tray of mango chutney and Indian-style pickles.

30 Rosemary, Bacon and Brie Muffins

Serves 8

75 g (3 oz) rindless streaky
  bacon rashers, finely chopped
225 g (7½ oz) plain flour
1½ teaspoons baking powder
1 teaspoon bicarbonate of soda
1 teaspoon sweet paprika
2 large eggs
¼ teaspoon black pepper
pinch of salt
2 teaspoons finely chopped
  rosemary
150 ml (¼ pint) milk
75 g (3 oz) butter, melted
125 g (4 oz) firm Brie cheese,
  cut into cubes

- Cook the bacon in a large frying pan over a high heat for 3–4 minutes, stirring occasionally, until golden. Drain on kitchen paper.

- Meanwhile, sift the flour into a large bowl with the baking powder, bicarbonate of soda and paprika.

- Break the eggs into a jug and beat lightly. Add the pepper, salt, rosemary, milk and melted butter and whisk together. Pour the mixture into the dry ingredients, add ²/₃ of both the Brie and cooked bacon and stir until barely combined.

- Butter a 12-hole muffin tin. Divide the mixture between the prepared holes, top with the remaining bacon and Brie and bake in a preheated oven, 200°C (400°F), Gas Mark 6, for 18–22 minutes, until risen and golden. Serve warm.

10 Rosemary and Brie Flatbreads

Melt 50 g (2 oz) butter in a small pan with 1 crushed garlic clove, 2 teaspoons chopped rosemary, 1 teaspoon sweet paprika and a generous pinch of black pepper. Warm gently until the butter begins to froth, then set aside. Meanwhile, toast 6 sandwich pitta breads, flatbreads or thick wraps until lightly golden, and slice 200 g (7 oz) Brie. Brush the top of each bread with the flavoured butter, add a few slices of Brie and serve straight away.

20 Rosemary and Brie Ciabatta

Make 3–4 incisions in the top of 6 ciabatta rolls, taking care not to cut all the way through. Place 100 g (3½ oz) softened butter in a bowl with 1 clove crushed garlic, 1 teaspoon sweet paprika, 2 teaspoons chopped rosemary and plenty of ground black pepper. Mash well with a fork. Spread the rosemary butter inside the ciabatta incisions, then push a small slice of firm Brie into each one. Wrap each roll loosely in foil and bake in a preheated oven, 180°C (350°F), Gas Mark 4, for about 12 minutes, opening the foil for the final 2 minutes. The rolls should be lightly golden and the cheese melted. Serve hot.

2⏱ Curried Moules Marinières

Serves 4

2 tablespoons vegetable oil

1 onion, halved and finely sliced

2.5 cm (1 inch) piece of fresh root
  ginger, peeled and chopped

1 garlic clove, finely sliced

1 tablespoon medium
  curry paste

250 ml (8 fl oz) lager or dry
  white wine

3 tablespoons coconut milk

1 kg (2 lb) mussels, debearded
  and scrubbed

salt and pepper

roughly chopped coriander,
  to garnish

- Heat the oil in a large saucepan and cook the onion for
  4–5 minutes, until beginning to soften. Add the ginger
  and garlic and cook for 2–3 minutes, until softened.

- Stir in the curry paste and heat for 1 minute. Pour in the lager
  or wine and coconut milk, season and stir to combine. Simmer
  for 3–4 minutes, then add the mussels and stir again.

- Cover the pan with a tight-fitting lid and simmer gently
  for 3–4 minutes, shaking the pan occasionally, until the
  mussels are open.

- Discard any mussels that have not opened, then spoon
  the remainder and their broth into warmed dishes. Garnish
  with the chopped coriander and serve immediately with
  a large bowl for the empty shells.

 Curried Mussel Chapattis

Heat 2 tablespoons vegetable oil in a large frying pan and add 2 halved and sliced shallots, 1 crushed garlic clove and 1 teaspoon finely grated root ginger. Cook for 3–4 minutes over a medium-low heat, until softened and lightly golden. Meanwhile, warm 4 chapattis according to the packet instructions. Stir 2 tablespoons mild curry paste into the shallots and stir over the heat for 1 minute. Pour 300 ml (½ pint) coconut milk into the pan and bring to the boil. Tip 450 g (14½ oz) cooked, shelled mussels into the pan and stir as they heat through. Take off the heat and sprinkle with 2 tablespoons chopped coriander. To serve, place the chapattis on plates and spoon the curried mussels on top.

 Mini Mussel and Coconut Curry Pots Make the curried mussels following the 10-minute recipe, increasing the coconut milk to 400 ml (14 fl oz), then stir in the coriander. Meanwhile, roll out 250 g (8 oz) puff pastry to the thickness of a £1 coin. Cut into 4 circles 1 cm (½ inch) larger than 4 ovenproof ramekins. Spoon the mussels and sauce into the ramekins and top each with a pastry circle, allowing it to overhang slightly. Brush with beaten egg, cut a slit in the top of the pastry and sprinkle with black mustard or onion seeds. Bake in a preheated oven, 200°C (400°F), Gas Mark 6, for 15–18 minutes.

30 Golden Fried Mozzarella Balls with Chilli Jam

Serves 4

20 chilled mini mozzarella balls, drained
2 tablespoons flour
1 large egg, lightly beaten
75 g (3 oz) breadcrumbs
oil, for deep-frying
sweet chilli jam, to serve

- Pat the mozzarella balls dry on kitchen paper.

- Place the flour, egg and breadcrumbs in 3 shallow dishes.

- Roll the mozzarella balls first in the flour, then in the egg and finally in the breadcrumbs, ensuring they are well coated. Arrange in a single layer on a baking sheet and place in the freezer for 15 minutes.

- Meanwhile, heat a 3.5 cm (1½ inch) depth of oil in a deep-sided frying pan or saucepan to 180–190°C (350–375°F), or until a cube of bread browns in 1 minute.

- Remove the baking sheet from the freezer and use a slotted spoon to carefully lower the mozzarella balls into the hot oil a few at a time. Cook for about 60 seconds, or until they are crisp and golden. Drain on kitchen paper and keep warm. Repeat with the remaining balls and serve hot with sweet chilli jam for dipping.

 Chilli Cheese Dip and Dippers

Place 2 teaspoons sweet paprika in a small bowl with 1 teaspoon dried oregano, ½ teaspoon dried garlic granules and a generous pinch of cayenne pepper, salt and black pepper. Brush 3 soft flour tortillas with a little vegetable oil and sprinkle over the prepared spice blend to coat lightly. Cut into triangles and arrange in a single layer on a large baking sheet. Bake in a preheated oven, 200°C (400°F), Gas Mark 6, for 6–7 minutes, until crisp and lightly golden.

Meanwhile, combine 150 g (5 oz) cream cheese in a bowl with 2 tablespoons sweet chilli jam and 2 teaspoons chopped chives. Transfer the baked dippers to a wire rack to crisp up, then serve with the chilli cheese dip.

 Baked Chilli Cheese Fondue

Remove any plastic packaging from a whole Camembert or Brie cheese in a wooden box. Return it to the wooden box and cut several small slits in the surface of the cheese. Push 1 sliced garlic clove into the slits with a few small thyme sprigs and 1 deseeded and sliced mild red chilli. Bake in a preheated oven, 200°C (400°F), Gas Mark 6, for 12–15 minutes, until the cheese is melting. Serve with lots of crusty bread and a bowl of chilli jam, if desired.

 # Warm Fig and Prosciutto Salad with Gorgonzola

Serves 4

2 tablespoons olive oil
2 banana shallots, finely chopped
2 garlic cloves, finely chopped
2 teaspoons raspberry vinegar
8 small, ripe but firm figs
100 g (3½ oz) Gorgonzola cheese
100 g (3½ oz) rocket leaves
8 wafer-thin slices of prosciutto-
style ham
salt and pepper
lightly crushed toasted hazelnuts,
to garnish (optional)

- Place the oil in a small frying pan over a medium-low heat. When hot, add the shallots and garlic and fry for 4–5 minutes, until softened. Remove from the heat and whisk in the raspberry vinegar plus a pinch of salt and pepper.

- Meanwhile, use a sharp knife to score a cross into the top of the figs. Prise them open and fill with the Gorgonzola. Place on a baking sheet, drizzle with a little oil and slide under a preheated medium-hot grill for 4–5 minutes, until melting and lightly coloured.

- Arrange the rocket leaves on 4 plates and top with the warm figs and slices of ham. Drizzle over the warm dressing and serve immediately, scattered with toasted hazelnuts, if desired, and a pinch of black pepper.

Melting Gorgonzola, Fig and Parma Parcels

Cut 2 ripe but firm figs into 4 thick slices. Place 4 slices of Parma ham on a clean work surface, spacing them well apart, and place 4 more slices on top at right angles to form crosses. Slice 125 g (4 oz) Gorgonzola and place in the centre of each cross, followed by 2 slices of fig. Scatter with a few lightly crushed, toasted hazelnuts, then fold the ham over the filling to form 4 parcels. Heat 1 tablespoon oil in a large, nonstick frying pan and cook the parcels for 3–4 minutes, turning once, until crisp and golden. Serve the parcels with a dressed rocket salad.

Crispy Gorgonzola and Cured Ham Flatbreads

Place 2 baking sheets in a preheated oven, 220°C (425°F), Gas Mark 7. Put 200 g (7 oz) plain flour into a bowl with ¾ teaspoon instant dried yeast and ½ teaspoon salt. Pour in 125 ml (4 fl oz) hand-hot water and 2 teaspoons olive oil. Mix to form a soft dough, then transfer to a floured work surface and knead for 5–8 minutes, until smooth. Divide into 4 equal pieces, then roll them into balls. Using a rolling pin, roll each ball into a really thin oval shape about 28 x 15 cm (11 x 6 inches). Place the flatbreads on the hot baking sheets, drizzle a teaspoon of olive oil over each one and sprinkle with a pinch of sea salt. Bake for 5–7 minutes, until the flatbreads are crisp. Top each one with 2 thin slices of Gorgonzola and 2 wafer-thin slices of cured ham, and serve immediately, scattered with a small handful of rocket leaves, if desired.

3⬤ Spiced Pear and Stilton Tarts with Watercress

Serves 4

25 g (1 oz) butter, melted, plus extra for greasing
300 g (10 oz) chilled puff pastry
flour, for dusting
2 ripe but firm pears, peeled and cored
¼ teaspoon ground cloves
pinch of ground allspice
¼ teaspoon ground black pepper
75 g (3 oz) Stilton
25 g (1 oz) walnut pieces
1 teaspoon thyme leaves
1 red chilli, deseeded and chopped (optional)

To serve

watercress
maple syrup (optional)

- Lightly grease a baking sheet. Roll out the pastry on a lightly floured work surface to the thickness of a £1 coin. Using a 12 cm (5 inch) saucer as a template, cut out 4 circles and place them on the prepared baking sheet.

- Brush the circles with the melted butter and, using the tip of a sharp knife and a slightly smaller saucer, score a 1 cm (½ inch) border around the edge of each one. Bake in a preheated oven, 200°C (400°F), Gas Mark 6, for about 8 minutes, until pale golden in colour.

- Meanwhile, combine the cloves, allspice and pepper in a bowl.

- Remove the pastries from the oven and arrange the pear slices on them, keeping within the border. Dust lightly with the spices, then crumble over the Stilton and sprinkle with the walnuts and thyme leaves. Dot with the chilli, if using.

- Return the pastries to the oven for a further 8–10 minutes, until crisp and golden. Serve with a handful of watercress leaves and drizzled with a little maple syrup, if desired.

 Stilton, Pear and Watercress Salad

Peel, core and slice 2 ripe, firm pears. Place a handful of watercress on 4 plates and top with the pears. Crumble over 100 g (3½ oz) Stilton and sprinkle with 25 g (1 oz) walnut pieces, 1 deseeded and finely chopped red chilli and 1 teaspoon thyme leaves. Whisk 3 tablespoons walnut oil with 2 teaspoons red wine vinegar and 1 teaspoon maple syrup. Serve the salad drizzled with the dressing.

 Warm Pears with Stilton and Watercress Peel, quarter and core 3 ripe but firm pears. Melt 50 g (2 oz) butter in a nonstick frying pan with 1 tablespoon maple syrup and 1 deseeded and finely chopped red chilli (optional) over a medium-low heat. Add the pear quarters and fry gently for 3–5 minutes, until tender and lightly caramelized. Sprinkle over the spices from the main recipe and toss gently for a further minute. Set aside to cool slightly.

Place a handful of watercress on 4 plates and arrange the warm pears on top. Drizzle with the warm dressing, scatter over 75 g (3 oz) crumbled Stilton and 25 g (1 oz) lightly crushed walnuts and serve immediately.

20 Winter Herb Pesto and Goats' Cheese Ravioli

Serves 4

2 tablespoons blanched hazelnuts
4 tablespoons chopped herbs, such as parsley, thyme, rosemary, sage
25 g (1 oz) rocket leaves
1 small garlic clove, chopped
100 ml (3½ fl oz) extra virgin olive oil
1 teaspoon lemon juice
2 tablespoons freshly grated hard goats' cheese or Parmesan cheese, plus extra to serve
300 g (10 oz) fresh ravioli or tortellini, such as butternut squash and herb
salt and pepper

- Place a dry frying pan over a medium heat and toast the hazelnuts for 4–5 minutes, shaking the pan frequently, until lightly golden. Transfer to a plate and set aside to cool.

- Place the herbs, rocket, garlic and cooled hazelnuts in a small food processor and pulse briefly until coarsely chopped. With the motor running, add the olive oil in a steady stream and blend until almost smooth.

- Scrape the pesto into a bowl, then stir in the lemon juice and grated cheese, and season to taste.

- Cook the ravioli in a large pan of salted boiling water for 2–3 minutes, or according to the packet instructions, until 'al dente'. Drain and divide between 4 shallow bowls.

- Drizzle with the pesto, then crumble or grate the extra cheese over the top to serve.

 Goats' Cheese, Hazelnut and Radicchio Salad Toast 2 tablespoons blanched hazelnuts as in the main recipe. Tip on to a chopping board and crush lightly with a rolling pin. Combine 2 tablespoons finely chopped mixed herbs in a small bowl with 1 finely chopped shallot, 1 teaspoon wholegrain mustard, 1 tablespoon sherry vinegar, 3 tablespoons olive oil and a pinch of salt and pepper. Arrange the leaves from 1 radicchio on 4 plates and crumble 100 g (3½ oz) hard goats' cheese over the salads. Sprinkle with the toasted hazelnuts and drizzle with the dressing to serve.

 Winter Pesto and Goats' Cheese Mini Muffins Toast 3 tablespoons hazelnuts, using 2 tablespoons to make the pesto following the main recipe. Sift 150 g (5 oz) plain flour into a bowl with 1 teaspoon baking powder and a pinch of salt. Roughly chop or crush the reserved hazelnuts and stir into the flour with a pinch of black pepper. Break 1 egg into a jug, add 75 ml (3 fl oz) milk, 50 ml (2 fl oz) olive oil and 2 tablespoons of the pesto and beat together. Pour into the flour, add 75 g (3 oz) finely diced hard goats' cheese and stir until barely combined. Grease 18 holes in 1 or 2 mini muffin tins or line them with paper cases. Fill with the muffin mixture and bake in a preheated oven, 190°C (375°F), Gas Mark 5, for 12–15 minutes, until risen and golden. Cool a little on a wire rack and serve warm.

10 Warm Scallop and Radicchio Salad with Chorizo

Serves 4

1 tablespoon olive oil

100 g (3½ oz) chorizo ring, thinly sliced

225 g (7½ oz) small roeless scallops

small head of radicchio, leaves separated

large handful of frisée lettuce leaves

For the dressing

1 small shallot, finely chopped

1 teaspoon Dijon mustard

2 tablespoons olive oil

2 teaspoons sherry or red wine vinegar

salt and pepper

- Put the oil into a frying pan, add the chorizo and cook over a medium-high heat for 2–3 minutes, until crisp. Remove with a slotted spoon and set aside.

- Return the pan to the heat and cook the scallops for 1–2 minutes, tossing them occasionally, until opaque and slightly caramelized.

- Meanwhile, whisk together the dressing ingredients.

- Arrange the salad leaves on 4 plates, top with the scallops and chorizo and drizzle with the dressing.

20 Pan-Fried Scallops with Chorizo

Cut a 125 g (4 oz) chorizo ring into slices about 1 cm (½ inch) thick. Place 16 roeless king scallops in a bowl with 16 raw, peeled king prawns. Combine 1 teaspoon finely grated lemon rind with 2 tablespoons olive oil and ¼ teaspoon chilli flakes (optional). Pour over the scallops and mix well to coat. Heat 1 tablespoon olive oil in a large frying pan and fry the chorizo for about 2 minutes, until coloured. Remove with a slotted spoon and set aside. Return the pan to the heat and cook the scallops and prawns for 2–4 minutes, turning occasionally, until just cooked and starting to caramelize. Set aside and keep warm for 1–2 minutes, then serve with the salad leaves and chorizo, as in the main recipe.

30 Grilled Streaky Scallop Skewers with Chorizo

Toss the chorizo and scallops from the 20-minute recipe with the dressing. Set aside to marinate for 10 minutes. Cut 8 thin, rindless streaky bacon rashers in half and wrap a scallop in each. Thread onto metal skewers, alternating them with the chorizo slices, and place on a foil-lined grill rack. Cook under a preheated medium-hot grill for 6–8 minutes, turning occasionally, until the scallops are opaque and the bacon is crisp and golden. Serve with the salad, as in the main recipe.

30 Beetroot Tarte Tatin with Goats' Cheese

Serves 4–6

2 tablespoons olive oil
2 garlic cloves, chopped
1 teaspoon thyme leaves
2 tablespoons balsamic vinegar
500 g (1 lb) cooked beetroot
(not pickled), sliced or cut into
thin wedges
flour, for dusting
250 g (8 oz) chilled puff pastry
125 g (4 oz) crumbly goats' cheese
thyme leaves or snipped chives,
to garnish

- Place the oil in an ovenproof frying pan over a medium-low heat and, when hot, fry the garlic and thyme for 1–2 minutes, until just softened. Pour in the vinegar and simmer gently for 1–2 minutes, until just sticky.

- Arrange the beetroot to fit snugly and attractively in the pan, then increase the heat slightly and cook for 4–5 minutes, until the underside begins to brown.

- Meanwhile, place the pastry on a floured work surface and roll into a circle about 1 cm (½ inch) larger than the pan.

- Lay the pastry over the pan, tucking the edges in neatly to cover the beetroot, and bake in a preheated oven, 200°C (400°F), Gas Mark 6, for 15–20 minutes, until the pastry is puffed and golden.

- Invert the tarte on to a large plate, then crumble over the goats' cheese and serve garnished with the thyme or chives.

---

1 Goats' Cheese and Beetroot Tartlets

Trim 4 small seeded or herb tortilla wraps so that they fit into a 4–hole Yorkshire pudding tin, but overhang slightly. Place in a preheated oven, 180°C (350°F), Gas Mark 4, for 2–3 minutes, until beginning to brown. Meanwhile, combine 300 g (10 oz) cooked and diced beetroot (not pickled) in a bowl with 125 g (4 oz) diced or crumbled goats' cheese, 1 teaspoon chopped chives and a pinch of salt and pepper. Spoon this mixture into the prepared tin and return to the oven for 2–3 minutes, until the cheese is beginning to melt and the tortillas are crisp and golden. Transfer to serving plates and serve drizzled with a little olive oil and some shop-bought balsamic glaze (available from supermarkets), accompanied by a rocket salad.

2 Individual Goats' Cheese and Beetroot Quiches

Unroll a 320 g (10¾ oz) sheet of chilled shortcrust pastry and use to line 4 greased, individual quiche tins. Fill the pastry cases with 175 g (6 oz) diced, cooked beetroot, 100 g (3½ oz) defrosted peas and 100 g (3½ oz) crumbled goats' cheese. Break 3 eggs into a jug, beat together, then mix in 3 tablespoons single cream and 1 teaspoon chopped thyme leaves. Pour into the filled cases and bake in a preheated oven, 220°C (425°F), Gas Mark 7, for 12–15 minutes, or until set and golden.

WIN-FIRE-POG

30 Leek and Chestnut Pancakes

Serves 4

50 g (2 oz) butter
2 leeks, sliced
125 g (4 oz) button mushrooms, finely sliced
50 g (2 oz) cooked chestnuts, crumbled
2 teaspoons chopped tarragon
75 ml (3 fl oz) dry cider
100 ml (3½ fl oz) single cream
50 g (2 oz) plain flour
150 ml (¼ pint) milk
1 large egg, lightly beaten
salt and pepper
mixed salad, to serve (optional)

- Melt half the butter in a frying pan and cook the leeks for 5–6 minutes, until soft and golden. Add the mushrooms, chestnuts and tarragon and cook for a further 4–5 minutes, until softened. Pour in the cider and simmer until completely evaporated. Stir in the cream, then season and simmer for 1 minute to thicken slightly. Take off the heat and keep warm. Meanwhile, sift the flour into a bowl with a pinch of salt. Make a well in the centre and pour in the milk and egg. Mix well, using a balloon whisk, until the batter is smooth.

- Melt a knob of the remaining butter in a nonstick frying pan or 24 cm (9½ inch) crêpe pan over a medium heat. Pour a quarter of the batter into the pan and swirl to spread out. Cook for 1–2 minutes, until set and lightly golden underneath. Flip and cook the other side for 30–60 seconds, until golden. Transfer to a plate and keep warm. Repeat to make another 3 pancakes with the remaining batter.

- Place the pancakes on warmed plates, fill with the leek and chestnut mixture, then fold and serve with a mixed salad.

 Leek and Chestnut Soda Breads

Place 15 g (½ oz) mixed, dried mushrooms in a pan with 200 ml (7 fl oz) boiling water. Simmer for 7–8 minutes, until softened. Drain, then roughly chop. Meanwhile, cook the leeks as above. Add 50 g (2 oz) cooked, chopped chestnuts and 1 teaspoon chopped tarragon and cook for a further minute. Stir in 100 g (3½ oz) cream cheese and the mushrooms, stirring until the cheese has melted. Spoon on to toasted soda bread and serve.

 Leek and Chestnut Filos

Brush 4 individual Yorkshire pudding or quiche tins with melted butter. Brush 4 x 30 cm (12 inch) square sheets of filo pastry with melted butter and cut each into 4 equal squares. Use these to line the prepared tins, arranging the squares at slightly different angles. Bake in a preheated oven, 200°C (400°F), Gas Mark 6, for about 8 minutes, until golden. Meanwhile, cook the creamy leek and chestnut filling by following the main recipe. Stir 75 g (3 oz) cream cheese into the mixture with the cream. Carefully transfer the pastry cases to plates. Spoon in the filling and serve immediately, sprinkled with grated Parmesan cheese, if desired.

Smoked Duck with Clementine and Walnut Salad

Serves 4

2 clementines
100 g (3½ oz) watercress, plus a handful of extra leaves, to garnish
50 g (2 oz) walnuts, lightly crushed
200 g (7 oz) smoked duck breast, sliced
pomegranate seeds, to garnish (optional)

For the dressing

2 tablespoons walnut oil
2 teaspoons raspberry vinegar
salt and pepper

- Cut away the peel and pith from the clementines. Cut the flesh into segments, discarding the membrane, but reserving the juice in a small bowl.

- Arrange the watercress on 4 plates and sprinkle with the clementine segments and the walnuts. Top with the smoked duck slices and garnish with the cress leaves and pomegranate seeds, if using.

- To make the dressing, whisk the oil and vinegar into the reserved clementine juice and season to taste. Drizzle over the salad and serve.

 Warm Duck, Clementine and Walnut Salad Prepare the clementines and dressing following the main recipe. Place 2 tablespoons olive oil in a frying pan over a medium heat. Generously season 175 g (6 oz) mini duck fillets and sprinkle with ½ teaspoon Szechuan pepper. Place in the hot pan and cook for 3–4 minutes, turning once, until cooked but still slightly pink. Transfer to a warm place to rest for 10 minutes. Slice the duck fillets and scatter over the salads with the walnuts and pomegranate seeds from the main recipe. Serve drizzled with the dressing.

Sliced Duck with Clementines Prepare the clementines as in the main recipe, reserving the juice. Remove any excess fat from 2 duck breasts, then score the flesh with a sharp knife and season with salt and pepper. Heat a dry frying pan and cook the duck breasts, skin-side down over a medium-high heat, for 8–10 minutes, until really golden. Lower the heat and pour in the reserved clementine juice. Turn and cook the breasts for a further 5–10 minutes, until the juices are slightly sticky and the flesh still pink. Transfer to a warm place to rest for 10 minutes, then slice thickly.

Arrange on plates with the salad leaves, clementine segments and walnuts, as in the main recipe. Serve drizzled with the warm clementine and duck juices.

30 ⏺ Ricotta and Winter Herb Gnocchi

Serves 4

3 tablespoons olive oil

1 onion, chopped

3 garlic cloves, chopped

75 g (3 oz) fresh breadcrumbs

1½ teaspoons grated lemon rind

3 tablespoons chopped herbs,
   such as thyme, parsley,
   rosemary, chives and sage

50 g (2 oz) firm cheese, such
   as Emmental or Cheddar,
   finely grated

400 g (13 oz) shop-bought gnocchi

100 g (3½ oz) frozen leaf spinach,
   defrosted and chopped

250 g (8 oz) ricotta cheese

4 tablespoons double cream

¼ teaspoon ground nutmeg

salt and pepper

- Heat 2 tablespoons of the oil in a frying pan and cook the onion and 2 of the garlic cloves over a medium heat for 5–6 minutes, stirring frequently, until softened.

- Meanwhile, combine the breadcrumbs in a bowl with the remaining garlic and oil, ½ teaspoon of the lemon rind, half the herbs, the grated cheese and seasoning. Mix well.

- Cook the gnocchi in a large pan of lightly salted boiling water for 1–3 minutes, or according to the packet instructions. Drain.

- Squeeze any excess moisture from the spinach and place in a bowl with the cooked onion and garlic, the ricotta, the remaining herbs and lemon rind, the cream and nutmeg. Beat together, then season to taste.

- Stir the gnocchi into the ricotta mixture and divide between 4 individual, shallow ovenproof dishes. Top with the breadcrumb mixture and bake in a preheated oven, 190°C (375°F), Gas Mark 5, for 15–20 minutes, or until bubbling and golden.

---

10 ◔ Golden Gnocchi with Winter Herb and Ricotta Dip

Heat 1 tablespoon oil in a frying pan over a medium heat. Tip in 400 g (13 oz) shop-bought gnocchi and cook for 5–7 minutes. Meanwhile, place 150 g (5 oz) ricotta in a bowl with 2 teaspoons chopped herbs, 1 teaspoon grated lemon rind, 2 tablespoons crème fraîche and salt and pepper. Mix until smooth, then divide between 4 small dishes. Place the gnocchi in 4 pasta bowls and serve accompanied by the dishes of ricotta dip.

20 ◔ Winter Herb and Ricotta Frittata

Fry the gnocchi in an ovenproof pan following the 10-minute recipe. Meanwhile, beat 4 eggs in a bowl with 150 g (5 oz) ricotta, 2 teaspoons chopped herbs and a generous pinch of salt and pepper. Pour the egg mixture over the gnocchi and cook on a medium-low heat for 6–7 minutes, until just set. Meanwhile, combine 50 g (2 oz) freshly made breadcrumbs with 2 teaspoons chopped parsley, 50 g (2 oz) finely grated Emmental cheese and 2 teaspoons olive oil. Mix well. Sprinkle 100 g (3½ oz) ricotta over the top of the frittata and top with the herby breadcrumbs. Slide under a preheated medium-hot grill for 3–4 minutes, until golden. Serve cut into wedges.

 # Skier's Cheese and Lardon Tart

Serves 4

1 tablespoon olive oil
200 g (7 oz) smoked bacon lardons or pancetta
375 g (12 oz) ready-rolled, chilled puff pastry
1 teaspoon fine cornmeal
3 tablespoons crème fraîche
1 onion, halved and thinly sliced
75 g (3 oz) Swiss cheese, such as Emmental, grated
½ teaspoon dried thyme
green salad, to serve (optional)

- Place the oil in a large frying pan over a medium heat and fry the lardons for 3–4 minutes, until cooked but not browned. Remove with a slotted spoon and drain on kitchen paper.

- Place the pastry on a baking sheet lightly dusted with the cornmeal. Spread the crème fraîche over it, leaving a 1 cm (½ inch) border all around the edge.

- Scatter the onion and cheese over the crème fraîche, followed by the lardons and finally the thyme. Bake in a preheated oven, 220°C (425°F), Gas Mark 7, for 12–15 minutes, until crisp and golden, then serve with a green salad, if desired.

 ### Skier's Cheese on Toast

Lightly toast 4 thick slices of sourdough or country-style bread. Meanwhile, place 4 tablespoons crème fraîche in a bowl and combine with 100 g (3½ oz) grated Swiss cheese, half a finely chopped onion and ½ teaspoon dried thyme. Top the toasted bread with a slice of cured ham, then spread the cheesy mixture thickly over the ham. Place on a foil-lined grill rack and slide under a preheated medium-hot grill for 3–5 minutes, until melting. Slide on to plates and serve with a small green salad.

 ### Skier's Cheese Soufflé

Melt 25 g (1 oz) butter in a saucepan over a low heat. Mix in 25 g (1 oz) plain flour to form a paste, then stir over the heat for 45 seconds. Take the pan off the heat and stir in 150 ml (¼ pint) milk a little at a time, until smooth. Return the pan to a low heat and cook the sauce, stirring constantly, until it thickens. Transfer to a large bowl and set aside to cool slightly. Meanwhile, whisk 2 egg whites in a large, clean bowl until they form soft peaks. Beat 100 g (3½ oz) cream cheese into the bowl of sauce with 75 g (3 oz) grated Swiss cheese, ½ teaspoon dried thyme, 2 egg yolks and 2 slices finely chopped cured ham. Gently fold the egg whites into the mixture, then spoon into 4 greased individual soufflé dishes. Place on a baking sheet and bake in a preheated oven, 200°C (400°F), Gas Mark 6, for 15–18 minutes, until risen and golden. Serve immediately.

Warm Potato and Mackerel Salad

Serves 4

400 g (13 oz) waxy new
  potatoes, halved
3 tablespoons olive oil
2 teaspoons red wine vinegar
1 tablespoon wholegrain mustard
1 banana shallot, finely chopped
1 tablespoon rinsed and thinly
  sliced cornichons
2 teaspoons rinsed and drained
  capers
125 g (4 oz) cherry tomatoes,
  halved
2 tablespoons Kalamata-style
  olives, drained
4 small mackerel fillets, boned
  and skin lightly scored
large handful of frisée lettuce
  leaves
salt and pepper

- Cook the new potatoes in a large pan of salted boiling water for 12–15 minutes, until just tender. Drain, return to the pan and toss with 2 tablespoons of the olive oil. Add all the remaining ingredients, except the mackerel and frisée, then season to taste. Set aside.

- Heat the remaining tablespoon of olive oil in a large, nonstick frying pan and cook the mackerel fillets, skin-side down, for 3–4 minutes, until the flesh turns white. Gently turn them over and cook for a further minute, until lightly golden. Remove from the pan and cool slightly before flaking the flesh.

- Arrange the frisée on serving plates and serve with the warm potato salad and flaked mackerel.

Quick Smoked Mackerel Pâté

Place 200 g (7 oz) peppered smoked mackerel fillets in a food processor with 2 tablespoons crème fraîche, 150 g (5 oz) full-fat cream cheese and 2 teaspoons lemon juice. Blitz until almost smooth, then transfer to a bowl and stir in 2 tablespoons finely chopped parsley or chives. Scatter a few thinly sliced cornichons over the top to garnish, and serve with rough oatcakes or freshly made toast.

Hot Smoked Mackerel and Potato Pâté

Place 300 g (10 oz) floury potatoes in a pan with 350 ml (12 fl oz) hot milk, 1 chopped garlic clove and a generous pinch of salt and pepper. Bring to the boil, then simmer for about 15 minutes, or until the potatoes are tender. Meanwhile, prepare the mackerel pâté following the 10-minute recipe. Drain the potatoes, reserving the milk, and mash until smooth. Beat the pâté into the potatoes with 2 tablespoons olive oil and enough of the reserved milk to create a soft, spreadable mixture. Spoon into bowls, garnish with sliced cornichons and chopped parsley, and serve warm with crusty bread or toast.

QuickCook

Hearty Soups and Stews

Recipes listed by cooking time

30

20

10

10 Red Pepper Soup with Spicy Caraway and Chickpea Salsa

Serves 4

1.2 kg (2 lb 7 oz) good-quality
   roasted red pepper soup
2 tablespoons olive oil
½ red onion, chopped
2 garlic cloves, chopped
1 red chilli, chopped (and
   deseeded if less heat preferred)
400 g (13 oz) can chickpeas,
   rinsed and drained
1 teaspoon caraway seeds
2 ripe but firm tomatoes,
   deseeded and diced
2 tablespoons chopped coriander
crusty bread, to serve

- Heat the soup in a large saucepan, according to the instructions on the carton.

- Meanwhile, make the salsa. Heat the olive oil in a frying pan and cook the onion, garlic and chilli over a medium heat for 5–6 minutes, until slightly softened. Add the chickpeas and caraway seeds, fry for 2 minutes, then stir in the tomatoes and take off the heat.

- Stir most of the salsa and half the coriander into the hot soup, then ladle into bowls. Top with the remaining salsa and coriander and serve immediately with crusty bread.

---

20 Spiced Pepper and Chickpea Stew

with Caraway Cut 2 red peppers, 1 yellow pepper and 1 red onion into chunks. Heat 2 tablespoons olive oil in a large pan and cook the peppers and onion over a medium-high heat for 7–8 minutes. Reduce the heat slightly and add 2 chopped garlic cloves, 1 chopped red chilli and 1 teaspoon caraway seeds and stir for 1–2 minutes more. Add 2 x 350 ml (12 fl oz) cartons fresh, spicy pasta sauce, 2 x 400 g (13 oz) cans rinsed and drained chickpeas and the grated rind of 1 lemon. Simmer for 7–8 minutes then ladle into dishes. Garnish with coriander and serve with steamed couscous, rice or pasta.

30 Harissa-Spiced Pepper and Chickpea Soup

Chickpea Soup Heat 2 tablespoons olive oil in a large saucepan and cook 2 diced red peppers and 1 chopped red onion over a medium-high heat for 7–8 minutes. Reduce the heat and stir in 1–2 tablespoons harissa paste (depending on heat desired), 2 tablespoons sun-dried tomato purée, 1 teaspoon caraway seeds and 1 teaspoon ground cumin. Stir over the heat for 1–2 minutes, then pour in 500 g (1 lb) passata, 500 ml (17 fl oz) hot vegetable stock and a 400 g (13 oz) can rinsed and drained chickpeas. Season generously, then cover and simmer gently for about 15 minutes, until the peppers are soft. Blend to desired consistency, then ladle into bowls and serve drizzled with a little chilli or olive oil and a scattering of toasted cumin seeds, if desired.

Chicken and Spinach Stew

Serves 4

625 g (1¼ lb) skinless, boneless
   chicken thigh, thinly sliced
2 teaspoons ground cumin
1 teaspoon ground ginger
2 tablespoons olive oil
1 tablespoon tomato purée
2 x 400 g (13 oz) cans cherry
   tomatoes
50 g (2 oz) raisins
250 g (8 oz) cooked Puy lentils
1 teaspoon grated lemon rind
150 g (5 oz) baby spinach
salt and pepper
freshly chopped parsley,
   to garnish (optional)
steamed couscous or rice,
   to serve (optional)

- Mix the chicken with the ground spices until well coated. Heat the olive oil in a large saucepan or flameproof casserole dish, then add the chicken and cook for 2–3 minutes, until lightly browned.

- Stir in the tomato purée, tomatoes, raisins, lentils and lemon rind, season and simmer gently for about 12 minutes, until thickened slightly and the chicken is cooked.

- Add the spinach and stir until wilted. Ladle the stew into bowls, then scatter with parsley and serve with steamed couscous or rice, if desired.

 Quick Spinach and Watercress Soup

Melt 25 g (1 oz) butter in a large saucepan and fry 1 chopped garlic clove and 2 chopped spring onions over a medium heat for 2–3 minutes. Add 175 g (6 oz) cooked, peeled new potatoes and 1 litre (1¾ pints) hot vegetable stock. Bring to a simmer, then add 150 g (5 oz) watercress and 200 g (7 oz) chopped spinach leaves. Heat for 1–2 minutes, then blend until smooth. Season, then add a pinch of ground nutmeg. Ladle into bowls and top each with crème fraîche and a dusting of grated nutmeg.

Chicken and Rice Soup with Lemon

Heat 2 tablespoons oil in a large saucepan and cook 4 sliced spring onions and 2 chopped garlic cloves over a medium heat for 2–3 minutes, to soften. Add 200 g (7 oz) thinly sliced, skinless chicken breast and cook for 3–4 minutes, until lightly browned all over. Add 150 g (5 oz) washed long-grain rice and stir to coat in the oil. Pour 1.2 litres (2 pints) of good-quality, hot chicken or vegetable stock into the pan, season with salt and pepper and a pinch of freshly grated nutmeg, then simmer for about 15 minutes, until the rice is tender. Stir 150 g (5 oz) mixture of chopped watercress and spinach leaves into the soup and stir for 1–2 minutes, until the leaves have wilted. Ladle into bowls and serve with lemon wedges.

WIN-HEAR-HIZ

2 Quick Carrot and Coriander Tagine

Serves 4

2 tablespoons olive oil
875 g (1¾ lb) carrots, sliced
2.5 cm (1 inch) piece of fresh root
  ginger, peeled and finely chopped
2 garlic cloves, sliced
2 teaspoons baharat or ras el hanout
1 teaspoon ground coriander
pinch of saffron threads (optional)
8 ready-to-eat dried apricots, sliced
1 preserved lemon, chopped
400 ml (14 fl oz) hot vegetable
  stock
chopped coriander, to garnish
steamed giant couscous, to serve

- Heat the oil in a large saucepan or flameproof casserole dish and cook the carrots, ginger and garlic for 5–6 minutes, until beginning to soften. Add the spices and apricots and stir for a minute before adding the preserved lemon and hot stock. Cover and simmer for 10–12 minutes, until tender.

- Ladle the tagine into bowls, sprinkle with the coriander and serve with giant couscous.

---

1 Carrot and Coriander Soup with Cumin Toasts

Pour 2 x 600 g (1 lb 3½ oz) containers shop-bought carrot and coriander soup into a large saucepan and warm over a medium-low heat. Meanwhile, put 3 tablespoons olive oil into a frying pan, add 2 teaspoons cumin seeds and place over a medium-low heat for 2–3 minutes, until the cumin starts to brown. Toast 4 seeded pitta breads, then drizzle half the cumin oil over them and cut into strips. Ladle the soup into bowls and garnish with chopped coriander. Drizzle the remaining cumin oil on top and serve at once with the cumin toasts.

3 Moroccan-Style Carrot and Coriander Soup

Heat 2 tablespoons olive oil in a large saucepan or flameproof casserole dish and add 1 chopped onion, 1 tablespoon peeled and chopped fresh root ginger and 2 chopped garlic cloves. Cook over a medium heat for 7–8 minutes, until softened. Stir in 1 teaspoon ras el hanout and 1 teaspoon ground coriander, then add 750 g (1½ lb) chopped carrots and 1 chopped sweet potato. Stir to coat, then pour in 1.2 litres (2 pints) hot vegetable or chicken stock. Cover and simmer over a medium heat for about 15 minutes, until the vegetables are tender. Blend the soup with a hand-held blender, then season to taste and ladle into bowls. Garnish with plenty of freshly chopped coriander to serve.

10 Quick Pea and Leek Soup

Serves 4

50 g (2 oz) butter
2 banana shallots, finely chopped
2 leeks, very thinly sliced
1 tablespoon chopped mixed
   herbs, such as sage, thyme,
   chives and parsley
100 ml (3½ fl oz) crème fraîche
1 litre (1¾ pints) good-quality
   boiling vegetable stock
350 g (11½ oz) frozen petit pois
salt and pepper

- Melt the butter in a large saucepan over a medium heat, then add the shallots and leeks and cook for 5–6 minutes, until softened.

- Meanwhile, stir the chopped herbs into the crème fraîche and set aside.

- Add the vegetable stock and petit pois to the leeks and simmer for 2–3 minutes, until the peas are just tender.

- Season to taste, then ladle into bowls and serve immediately with a dollop of herby crème fraîche.

20 Potato, Pea and Leek Soup

Heat 2 tablespoons olive oil in a large saucepan or flameproof casserole dish and add 875 g (1¾ lb) diced potatoes, 2 chopped leeks and 3 thinly sliced spring onions. Cook over a medium heat for 5 minutes, stirring frequently, until the leek is beginning to soften. Add 1.2 litres (2 pints) boiling vegetable or chicken stock, season and simmer over a medium heat for about 12 minutes, until the potato is tender, adding 150 g (5 oz) frozen peas for the final 2–3 minutes. Blend the soup until smooth, then ladle into bowls and serve with the herby crème fraîche, as above, if desired.

30 Winter Potato, Pea and Leek Stew

Melt 25 g (1 oz) butter with 1 tablespoon olive oil in a large saucepan or flameproof casserole dish. Add 3 thickly sliced leeks and 2 chopped garlic cloves and cook for 4–5 minutes, until beginning to soften. Meanwhile, chop 500 g (1 lb) potatoes and 300 g (10 oz) sweet potatoes into chunks. Add to the pan with 50 g (2 oz) pearled spelt or pearl barley, 400 ml (14 fl oz) boiling vegetable stock, 1 rosemary sprig and 2 thyme sprigs. Season with a pinch of salt and plenty of black pepper, and simmer for 20–22 minutes, adding 200 g (7 oz) frozen peas for the final 3–4 minutes. When everything is tender, discard the herb sprigs and ladle the stew into deep dishes. Garnish with chives and serve with crusty bread.

WIN-HEAR-ZOY

30 Chinese-Style Beef and Ginger Casserole

Serves 4

2 tablespoons vegetable oil

1 onion, halved and sliced

2.5 cm (1 inch) piece root ginger, peeled and cut into matchsticks

2 garlic cloves, sliced

3 spring onions, sliced diagonally

1 teaspoon Chinese five spice

½ teaspoon chilli flakes (optional)

1 star anise

3 tablespoons oyster sauce

2 tablespoons light soy sauce

1½ tablespoons cornflour, mixed with 1 tablespoon water

600 ml (1 pint) beef stock

500 g (1 lb) fillet or rump steak, thinly sliced

175 g (6 oz) mangetout, shredded

steamed Thai rice, to serve

- Heat half the oil in a large saucepan and stir-fry the onion over a medium heat for 4–5 minutes, until softened. Add the ginger, garlic and spring onions, and fry for 2–3 minutes, until softened slightly. Reduce the heat to low, add the spices and cook for 1–2 minutes, until aromatic.

- Combine the oyster sauce and soy sauce, add to the cornflour mixture, then stir into the stock and bring to the boil. Simmer for 10 minutes, stirring occasionally.

- Meanwhile, heat the remaining oil in a hot wok or frying pan and stir-fry the beef over a high heat for 3–4 minutes, until browned all over. Set aside.

- Add the mangetout to the stock, simmer for 2–3 minutes, then add the beef. Spoon into bowls and serve immediately with steamed Thai rice.

---

10 Beef and Ginger Soupy Noodles

Heat 1.2 litres (2 pints) clear beef stock in a saucepan and add a 3.5 cm (1½ inch) piece fresh root ginger cut into matchsticks, 1 sliced red chilli and 2 tablespoons dark soy sauce. Simmer for 2–3 minutes, then add 600 g (1 lb 3½ oz) straight-to-wok thick noodles and simmer for 2 minutes more. Add 350 g (11½ oz) thinly sliced fillet steak, 100 g (3½ oz) shredded mangetout and 50 g (2 oz) bean sprouts and cook for 1–2 minutes, until the meat colours. Ladle into bowls to serve.

20 Ginger Beef Broth with Winter

Greens Cut 500 g (1 lb) sirloin or rump steak into very thin slices, cutting against the grain. Place in a bowl with 1 tablespoon peeled and grated fresh root ginger, 1 crushed garlic clove, 1 finely chopped red chilli (optional) and 1 teaspoon minced lemon grass. Mix well, then set aside to marinate for 5 minutes. Heat 2 tablespoons vegetable oil in a large saucepan or wok and stir-fry the marinated beef for 3–4 minutes over a medium-high heat, until aromatic. Add

750 ml (1¼ pints) good-quality hot beef stock, 3 tablespoons oyster sauce and 2 tablespoons light soy sauce and simmer for 2–3 minutes. Tip 250 g (8 oz) shredded winter or spring greens into the pan and simmer for 3–4 minutes, until wilted. Ladle into bowls and top each one with a small handful of bean sprouts to serve.

Quick Parsnip and Lentil Dhal

Serves 4–6

300 g (10 oz) split red lentils
2 tablespoons vegetable oil
1 onion, finely chopped
2 garlic cloves, crushed
1 tablespoon peeled and grated fresh root ginger
2 teaspoons mild curry powder
1 teaspoon garam masala
½ teaspoon ground turmeric
500 g (1 lb) parsnips, diced
400 ml (14 fl oz) hot vegetable stock
2 tablespoons coconut cream
150 g (5 oz) spinach leaves, roughly chopped
salt and pepper
naan bread, to serve

- Cook the lentils in a pan of boiling water for 15 minutes, or according to the packet instructions, until tender.

- Meanwhile, heat the vegetable oil in a large saucepan and cook the onion, garlic and ginger for 5–6 minutes over a medium heat, stirring frequently, until starting to colour. Add the spices and parsnips, cook for 1 minute, then add the stock and coconut cream and cook for about 10 minutes, until tender.

- Drain the lentils and add to the stock pan. Add the spinach and stir for 1 minute, until wilted. Season to taste, then spoon into bowls and serve with naan bread.

Lentil Soup with Spiced Parsnip Croûtons

Heat 2 tablespoons vegetable oil in a large saucepan over a medium-high heat and cook 1 grated red onion, 2 crushed garlic cloves and 2 teaspoons peeled and grated fresh root ginger for 4–5 minutes, until softened. Meanwhile, heat 2 tablespoons vegetable oil in a frying pan and fry 250 g (8 oz) finely diced parsnips over a medium-high heat for 7–8 minutes, turning frequently, until tender and golden. Drain on kitchen paper. Add the spices from the main recipe to the onion mixture and cook for 1 minute. Now add 2 x 400 g (13 oz) cans rinsed and drained green lentils in water and 1.2 litres (2 pints) boiling vegetable stock. Simmer for 3–4 minutes, until really tender, then blend to desired consistency. Ladle into bowls and serve topped with the golden parsnip croûtons.

Curried Parsnip and Lentil Soup

Heat 2 tablespoons oil in a large saucepan and cook 1 chopped onion, 2 chopped garlic cloves and 1 tablespoon peeled and grated fresh root ginger for 4–5 minutes over a medium-high heat until starting to colour. Reduce the heat then stir in the spices from the main recipe, 125 g (4 oz) split red lentils and 875 g (1¾ lb) chopped parsnips. Cook for 1 minute, then add 1.3 litres (2¼ pints) hot vegetable stock and 200 ml (7 fl oz) coconut milk. Cover and simmer for 15 minutes. Blend, season and serve with naan.

WIN-HEAR-DOH

30 Lamb and Gnocchi Hotpot

Serves 4

3 tablespoons olive oil
500 g (1 lb) cubed lamb
1 onion, chopped
2 garlic cloves, chopped
1 bay leaf
1 tablespoon chopped fresh
  oregano, plus extra leaves
  to serve
2 tablespoons tomato purée
125 ml (4 fl oz) red wine
2 x 400 g (13 oz) cans cherry or
  chopped tomatoes
1 teaspoon grated lemon rind
400 g (13 oz) fresh potato
  gnocchi
75 g (3 oz) feta cheese, crumbled
salt

- Heat 2 tablespoons of oil in a large, flameproof frying pan or casserole over a high heat and fry the lamb for 2–3 minutes, until browned all over. Transfer to a plate and set aside.

- Reduce the heat slightly, then fry the onion and garlic over a medium heat for 3–4 minutes, until beginning to soften. Add the bay leaf, oregano and tomato purée and stir over the heat for 1 minute. Pour in the red wine, boil for 1 minute, then add the tomatoes and lemon rind and simmer for 5–6 minutes, to thicken slightly. Return the lamb to the pan and simmer for a further 5–6 minutes, until just cooked.

- Meanwhile, cook the gnocchi in a pan of salted boiling water for 1–2 minutes, or according to the packet instructions. Drain. Arrange the gnocchi on top of the lamb mixture. Sprinkle with the feta, then drizzle with the remaining oil. Slide under a preheated, medium-hot grill for 4–5 minutes, until golden. Garnish with extra oregano leaves.

 Lamb Ratatouille with Golden Gnocchi Heat 2 tablespoons oil in a frying pan and brown 4 lamb leg steaks over a high heat for 1 minute on each side. Add 125 ml (4 fl oz) red wine and simmer to reduce by half. Add 2 x 400 g (13 oz) cans ratatouille, then simmer for 3–5 minutes, until the steaks are cooked. Meanwhile, heat 1 tablespoon oil in a frying pan and fry 400 g (13 oz) fresh potato gnocchi over a medium heat for 3–5 minutes. Serve with the ratatouille, topped with oregano and crumbled feta, if desired.

Baked Lamb Gnocchi Cook 400 g (13 oz) fresh potato gnocchi in a large pan of boiling salted water for 1–2 minutes, or according to the packet instructions, then drain. Meanwhile, heat 2 tablespoons olive oil in a large, flameproof frying pan or casserole dish and brown 4 thick lamb leg steaks for 1 minute on each side. Add 2 x 400 g (13 oz) cans good-quality ratatouille and a 400 g (13 oz) can rinsed and drained flageolet beans (optional) and bring to the boil. Top with an even layer of the gnocchi, then scatter over 75 g (3 oz) crumbled feta and 1 teaspoon dried oregano. Drizzle with 1 tablespoon olive oil, then transfer the pan to a preheated oven, 200°C (400°F), Gas Mark 6, for 12–15 minutes, until the gnocchi is golden. Remove and serve with a Greek-style salad.

20 Jerk Chicken and Sweet Potato Soup

Serves 4–6

2 tablespoons vegetable oil

1 red onion, chopped

1 celery stick, chopped

2.5 cm (1 inch) piece of fresh root ginger, peeled and chopped

1 tablespoon jerk seasoning

1 kg (2 lb) sweet potato, chopped (or use a mixture of sweet potato and butternut squash)

1.2 litres (2 pints) hot chicken stock

2 tablespoons lime juice

250 g (8 oz) cooked chicken, shredded

salt and pepper

thinly sliced spring onions, to garnish

- Heat the vegetable oil in a large pan and fry the onion, celery and ginger for 4–5 minutes, until beginning to soften. Add the jerk seasoning, then mix in the sweet potato and stir over the heat for 1 minute.

- Pour the chicken stock into the pan and simmer over a medium heat for about 12 minutes, until the potato is tender. Blend to the desired consistency, then stir in the lime juice and season to taste.

- Ladle the soup into bowls and top each with a handful of the shredded chicken. Garnish with spring onions and serve.

10 Quick Jerk Chicken Broth

Heat 2 tablespoons oil in a large saucepan over a medium heat and add 3 sliced spring onions and 1 tablespoon peeled and grated root ginger. Cook for 1–2 minutes until softened. Stir in 1 tablespoon jerk spice mix and cook for 1 minute before pouring in 1.2 litres (2 pints) hot chicken stock. Simmer for 3–4 minutes, then take off the heat and stir in 250 g (8 oz) shredded cooked chicken and 1–2 tablespoons lime juice. Ladle into bowls and serve, garnished with extra sliced spring onions, if desired.

30 Jerk Chicken and Sweet Potato

Curry Coat 500 g (1 lb) diced chicken thigh in 1½ tablespoons jerk spice mix or paste and set aside. Heat 2 tablespoons vegetable oil in a large pan over a medium-high heat and fry 1 chopped onion, 1 large chopped red pepper, 2 chopped garlic cloves and 2 teaspoons peeled and chopped fresh root ginger for 6–7 minutes, until softened. Add the chicken to the pan and stir frequently for 2–3 minutes, until browned all over. Add 600 g (1 lb 3½ oz) chopped sweet potato and stir to coat.

Pour in 500 ml (17 fl oz) hot chicken stock and simmer gently over a medium heat for 12–15 minutes, until the chicken is cooked and the potato tender. Serve spooned over plain or coconut rice, garnished with sliced spring onions.

WIN-HEAR-SAB

3O Spicy Black-Eyed Beans and Bangers

Serves 4

6 thick, Italian-style spicy sausages
1 tablespoon olive oil
225 g (7½ oz) chorizo, cubed
2 leeks, thickly sliced
1 celery stick, finely sliced
2 garlic cloves, chopped
125 ml (4 fl oz) dry white wine
400 ml (14 fl oz) hot chicken or
    vegetable stock
2 teaspoons freshly chopped sage
1 tablespoon wholegrain mustard
400 g (13 oz) can black-eyed
    beans, rinsed and drained
crusty bread, to serve (optional)

- Grill the sausages under a preheated hot grill for 5–6 minutes, turning occasionally, until browned. Set aside to cool slightly.

- Meanwhile, heat the oil in a large saucepan or flameproof casserole dish and add the chorizo, leeks and celery. Cook for 4–5 minutes over a medium heat until slightly softened. Add the garlic and cook for a further 2 minutes. Pour the wine into the pan and boil to reduce by half. Add the stock, sage, mustard and beans and return to the boil.

- Once the sausages are cool enough to handle, slice them. Add to the saucepan and simmer gently for 15 minutes, until cooked through and the sauce has thickened slightly.

- Spoon into dishes and serve with lots of crusty bread.

 Black-Eyed Bean Soup with Sizzled Sausages Melt 50 g (2 oz) butter in a saucepan and cook 2 chopped leeks and 1 chopped celery stick over a medium heat for 4–5 minutes. Meanwhile, remove the casings from 3 spicy sausages. Heat 1 tablespoon oil in a frying pan and fry the sausages over a high heat, breaking them up as they cook, until crisp and golden. Add 2 chopped garlic cloves to the leek mixture, heat for 2 minutes, then add 2 x 400 g (13 oz) cans rinsed and drained black-eyed beans and 1.2 litres (2 pints) hot vegetable stock. Bring to the boil, then blend. Ladle the soup into bowls and serve topped with the sausagemeat.

 Sausage and Black-Eyed Bean Soup Grill 6 spicy sausages under a medium-hot grill for 12–14 minutes, turning occasionally, until cooked and golden. Meanwhile, melt 50 g (2 oz) butter in a large saucepan and cook 2 thinly sliced leeks and 2 finely chopped celery sticks over a medium heat for 5–6 minutes, until beginning to soften. Add 2 chopped garlic cloves and cook for a further 2 minutes. Pour 125 ml (4 fl oz) dry white wine into the pan and boil to completely evaporate. Add a 400 g (13 oz) can rinsed and drained black-eyed beans, 1 tablespoon chopped sage and 1 litre (1¾ pints) hot stock and simmer for 7–8 minutes, until everything is tender. Slice the sausages thickly and divide between 4 bowls. Ladle over the soup and serve, garnished with freshly chopped parsley.

20 Coconut Fish Laksa with Lemon Grass

Serves 4

3 tablespoons laksa paste
(if unavailable, use Thai red
curry paste)

400 ml (14 fl oz) coconut milk

400 ml (14 fl oz) hot vegetable
stock

2 teaspoons fish sauce

2 lemon grass stalks, finely sliced
(woody outer leaves discarded)

250 g (8 oz) ribbon rice noodles

625 g (1¼ lb) white fish fillet
chunks, any bones removed

150 g (5 oz) bean sprouts

To garnish (optional)
coriander leaves
1 sliced red chilli

- Place the laksa paste and coconut milk in a large saucepan and bring to the boil. Simmer for 2–3 minutes, then add the stock, fish sauce and lemon grass and simmer for a further 5 minutes.

- Meanwhile, soak the rice noodles according to the packet instructions, until tender.

- Stir the chunks of fish into the soup and continue to simmer gently for 3–4 minutes, until cooked. Add the bean sprouts and take off the heat.

- Drain the noodles and heap into bowls. Ladle over the soup and serve the laksa garnished with coriander leaves and sliced red chilli, if desired.

10 Quick Prawn and Coconut Soupy Noodles

Place 2 tablespoons laksa or Thai red curry paste in a hot pan with 400 ml (14 fl oz) coconut milk, 1 teaspoon lemon grass paste, 1 litre (1¾ pints) vegetable stock and 2 tablespoons fish sauce. Bring to the boil and simmer for 4–5 minutes. Add 300 g (10 oz) cooked peeled prawns and 375 g (12 oz) cooked rice noodles. Simmer for 2 minutes, until the noodles are soft and the prawns hot. Ladle the soupy noodles into bowls and serve garnished as above, if desired.

30 Eastern Coconut Fish Stew

Heat 2 tablespoons vegetable oil in a large saucepan and cook 3 sliced banana shallots for 3–4 minutes, until softened and lightly coloured. Add 2 crushed garlic cloves, 2 teaspoons peeled and finely grated fresh root ginger and 2 finely chopped lemon grass hearts and stir-fry for a further 2 minutes. Add 3 tablespoons laksa paste or Thai red curry paste and 3 tablespoons coconut milk from a 400 ml (14 fl oz) can and cook over a medium heat for 2–3 minutes. Add the remaining coconut milk plus 300 ml (½ pint) chicken or fish stock and 2 shredded lime leaves or the finely grated rind of 1 lime. Bring to the boil, then simmer for about 10 minutes. Cut 400 g (13 oz) chunky, boneless white fish fillets into bite-sized pieces and add to the pan with 200 g (7 oz) raw peeled king prawns. Simmer for 3–4 minutes, until cooked through. Serve with sticky rice and garnished as above, if desired.

10 Mulligatawny in a Mug

Serves 4–6

2 tablespoons vegetable oil
1 onion, coarsely grated
1 garlic clove, crushed
3 tablespoons medium-hot
   curry paste
½ teaspoon ground turmeric
1 litre (1¾ pints) hot chicken stock
1 small apple, peeled and grated
500 g (1 lb) cooked basmati rice
350 g (11½ oz) cooked chicken,
   torn into bite-sized pieces
100 g (3½ oz) small croûtons
chopped coriander, to garnish

- Heat the oil in a large saucepan and cook the onion and garlic for 3–4 minutes over a medium-high heat, stirring frequently, until softened.

- Add the curry paste and turmeric, stir for 1 minute, then add the stock, apple and rice. Simmer for 3–4 minutes to thicken slightly.

- Stir in the chicken, then ladle the mulligatawny into wide mugs. Top with the croûtons and the coriander.

20 Quick Chicken Mulligatawny

Heat 2 tablespoons oil in a large saucepan and add 1 chopped onion, 2 chopped garlic cloves, 1 chopped carrot and 2 chopped potatoes. Cook over a medium heat for 6–7 minutes, stirring frequently. Stir in 2 tablespoons Madras-style curry paste and cook for 1 minute. Add 1.2 litres (2 pints) hot chicken stock and 1 small, peeled and grated apple. Bring to the boil and simmer for 8–10 minutes, until tender. Blend to desired consistency, or leave chunky, then stir in 250 g (8 oz) cooked basmati rice and 250 g (8 oz) shredded cooked chicken. Ladle into bowls and serve garnished with croûtons and coriander, if desired.

30 Chicken Mulligatawny-Style Stew

Heat 2 tablespoons vegetable oil in a large saucepan and cook 1 roughly chopped onion and 1 red pepper for 5–6 minutes, until beginning to soften. Add 2 crushed garlic cloves and 2 teaspoons peeled and grated fresh root ginger and cook for a further minute. Add 3 tablespoons Madras-style curry paste and cook for 1 more minute. Cut 500 g (1 lb) boneless, skinless chicken thighs into bite-sized pieces and add to the pan along with 100 g (3½ oz) split red lentils. Cook for 2–3 minutes, stirring frequently, until the chicken changes colour. Pour in 500 ml (17 fl oz) boiling chicken stock, then add 1 small, peeled and grated apple and 2 diced potatoes. Bring to the boil and cook for 15–18 minutes, until the vegetables and lentils are tender. Serve with steamed basmati rice and garnish with chopped coriander.

30 Lazy Winter Vegetable Hotpot

Serves 4–6

750 g (1½ lb) small waxy
   potatoes, peeled
25 g (1 oz) butter
1 onion, chopped
2 garlic cloves, chopped
500 ml (17 fl oz) good-quality,
   boiling vegetable or lamb stock
3 parsnips, cut into chunks
1 small celeriac, peeled and cut
   into chunks
3 carrots, sliced 1 cm
   (½ inch) thick
2 leeks, thickly sliced
1 tablespoon chopped rosemary
2 tablespoons olive oil
salt and pepper
finely chopped curly parsley,
   to garnish (optional)

- Cook the potatoes in a large pan of salted boiling water for 8–10 minutes, until just tender. Drain well and set aside to cool slightly.

- Meanwhile, melt the butter in a large saucepan or flameproof casserole dish and cook the onion and garlic over a medium heat for about 5 minutes, until slightly softened and coloured.

- Pour in the stock and add the prepared vegetables and rosemary. Season with a pinch of salt and pepper, then cover and simmer over a medium heat for 15–20 minutes, until the vegetables are tender.

- Once the potatoes are cool enough to handle, slice thickly. Heat the oil in a large, nonstick frying pan and fry the potatoes over a medium heat for 10–12 minutes, turning occasionally, until crisp and golden. Drain on kitchen paper.

- Ladle the vegetable hotpot into shallow bowls, top with the potato slices and serve immediately, garnished with freshly chopped parsley, if desired.

---

10 Cream of Vegetable Soup

Bring 1.2 litres (2 pints) good-quality vegetable stock to the boil with 1 rosemary sprig. Add 1 kg (2 lb) mixed frozen vegetables plus a pinch of salt and pepper and simmer for 5–6 minutes, until the vegetables are tender. Discard the rosemary and blend the soup to desired consistency, adding a little extra liquid if necessary. Ladle into bowls, drizzle 1 tablespoon single cream over each and add a small pinch freshly grated nutmeg to serve.

20 Winter Vegetable Soup

Heat 50 g (2 oz) butter in a large saucepan and cook 2 chopped leeks over a medium heat for 3–4 minutes, until beginning to soften. Add 1 kg (2 lb) mixed, finely chopped winter vegetables, such as squash, potatoes, carrots and parsnips (the chopping can be done in a food processor if you like). Cook for a further 2–3 minutes. Add 1.2 litres (2 pints) boiling vegetable stock, season with a pinch of salt and pepper, then cover and simmer rapidly for 10–12 minutes, or until the vegetables are just tender. Blend to desired consistency, adding more liquid if necessary, then ladle into deep bowls. Serve immediately, drizzled with rosemary oil or olive oil and sprinkled with grated pecorino cheese.

30 Peperonata-Style Pork and Chorizo Casserole

Serves 4

2 tablespoons olive oil
450 g (14½ oz) pork fillet, cubed
125 g (4 oz) chorizo sausage, diced
1 red pepper, deseeded and sliced
1 onion, halved and sliced
2 garlic cloves, chopped
150 g (5 oz) mushrooms, sliced
1 tablespoon sweet smoked paprika
450 g (14½ oz) potatoes, cubed
400 g (13 oz) can chopped
   tomatoes
175 ml (6 fl oz) hot vegetable stock
2 tablespoons chopped parsley
salt and pepper
boiled long-grain rice, to serve
100 ml (3½ fl oz) soured cream,
   to serve

- Heat the olive oil in a large, deep-sided frying pan and brown the pork over a medium-high heat for 2–3 minutes, turning occasionally. Add the chorizo, cook for 1 minute, then transfer all the meat to a plate and set aside.

- Cook the pepper and onion in the same pan for 3–4 minutes, until beginning to soften. Add the garlic and mushrooms and cook for a further 2–3 minutes, to soften slightly.

- Stir in the paprika and potatoes and heat for 1 minute. Add the tomatoes and stock and simmer for about 12 minutes, until the potato is almost tender.

- Return the meat to the pan and cook for 5–6 minutes more, until the pork is cooked but still juicy. Season to taste.

- Scatter the goulash with chopped parsley. Serve in dishes with cooked long-grain rice and dollops of soured cream.

 Chunky Chorizo and Peperonata

Pots Heat 2 tablespoons olive oil in a large frying pan and fry 400 g (13 oz) pork stir-fry strips over a medium-high heat for 2–3 minutes, until browned. Add 225 g (7½ oz) diced chorizo and cook for 1–2 minutes, until golden, then add 150 g (5 oz) quartered mushrooms and cook for 2–3 minutes, until softened. Drain a 280 g (9¼ oz) jar sliced, mixed roasted peppers, add to the pan and stir to heat through. Serve immediately with rice, soured cream and a sprinkling of chopped parsley.

 Chorizo Peperonata with

Pork Place 3 tablespoons olive oil in a large frying pan over a medium heat and fry 2 sliced red peppers, 1 sliced yellow or orange pepper and 1 sliced red onion for 3–4 minutes. Reduce the heat slightly and add 75 g (3 oz) thinly shredded sliced chorizo, 1 teaspoon chopped thyme and a generous pinch of salt and pepper. Cook for a further 10 minutes, stirring occasionally, adding 2 thinly sliced garlic cloves for the final 3–4 minutes. When everything is softened and lightly coloured, stir in 2 ripe diced tomatoes and 2 teaspoons sherry or balsamic vinegar and heat for a further 1–2 minutes, until the tomatoes begin to collapse. Meanwhile, heat 2 tablespoons olive oil in a large frying pan and cook 4 seasoned pork chops for about 10 minutes, turning once, until cooked through but still juicy. Place on 4 warmed plates and serve with the chorizo peperonata.

WIN-HEAR-XUP

10 Quick Mushroom and Garlic Tom Yum

Serves 4

1 tablespoon tom yum paste
1 litre (1¾ pints) vegetable stock
150 g (5 oz) oyster mushrooms, sliced
200 g (7 oz) closed-cup mushrooms, sliced
100 g (3½ oz) enoki mushrooms (optional)
2 spring onions, thinly sliced
2 garlic cloves, sliced
2.5 cm (1 inch) piece fresh root ginger, peeled and sliced
lime juice, to serve

- Place the tom yum paste in a large saucepan with the stock and bring to a simmer. Add the mushrooms, spring onions, garlic and ginger and simmer for 5–6 minutes, so the flavours develop and the mushrooms soften.

- Ladle into bowls and serve immediately with a squeeze of lime juice.

20 Wild Mushroom and Garlic Broth

Place 25 g (1 oz) mixed dried mushrooms in a pan with 1 litre (1¾ pints) just simmering water. Cover and cook for 10 minutes, until softened. Meanwhile, heat 2 tablespoons oil in a saucepan and cook 1 diced celery stick, 1 sliced leek, 2 chopped shallots and 2 chopped garlic cloves for 7–8 minutes over a medium heat until softened. Add 300 g (10 oz) sliced portobello mushrooms and cook for a further 2 minutes, until just beginning to soften. Strain the dried mushrooms, reserving the liquid, then slice and add to the vegetables. Stir, then add the reserved mushroom stock and simmer for 4–5 minutes. Ladle into bowls and serve.

30 Roasted Garlic Mushroom Soup

Arrange 600 g (1 lb 3½ oz) portobello or large field mushrooms, stalk-side up, in a shallow ovenproof dish. Place 50 g (2 oz) softened butter in a bowl with 1 small crushed garlic clove, 2 tablespoons chopped parsley and a pinch of salt and pepper. Mash together with a fork, then smear over the mushrooms. Roast in a preheated oven, 200°C (400°F), Gas Mark 6, for about 15 minutes, until softened and aromatic. Meanwhile, melt 25 g (1 oz) butter in a large saucepan with 1 tablespoon olive oil and fry 1 chopped celery stick, 1 chopped potato, 1 sliced leek and 2 teaspoons freshly chopped thyme leaves over a medium-low heat, stirring occasionally, for 10–12 minutes, until softened. Pour in 800 ml (1 pint 7 fl oz) hot beef or vegetable stock, increase the heat slightly and simmer for a further 5–6 minutes, until the vegetables are tender. Remove the roasted mushrooms from the oven, add to the pan and simmer for 2–3 minutes. Blend the soup to the desired texture, then ladle into bowls and serve with crusty bread.

WIN-HEAR-RYN

30 King Prawn and Sweet Potato Curry

Serves 4

2 tablespoons vegetable oil
1 large onion, chopped
2 garlic cloves, sliced
1 tablespoon peeled and chopped
  fresh root ginger
1 green chilli, thinly sliced
3 tablespoons mild curry paste
400 g (13 oz) sweet potato, diced
400 ml (14 fl oz) coconut milk
250 ml (8 fl oz) vegetable stock
small handful of curry leaves
400 g (13 oz) king prawns
100 g (3½ oz) frozen leaf spinach,
  defrosted and drained

To serve

steamed pilau rice or naan bread
coriander leaves, freshly chopped

- Heat the oil in a large, deep-sided frying pan or wok and cook the onion over a medium-high heat for 3–4 minutes, until beginning to colour. Add the garlic, ginger and chilli and stir-fry for a further 2 minutes. Reduce the heat slightly and add the curry paste, stirring for 1–2 minutes.

- Add the sweet potato dice, tossing them to coat, then add the coconut milk, stock and curry leaves. Simmer gently for 12–15 minutes, until the sweet potato is almost tender.

- Add the prawns and spinach and stir over the heat for 2–3 minutes, until the prawns are just cooked through.

- Spoon the curry into dishes, and serve immediately with steamed pilau rice or naan, and chopped coriander.

10 Curried Prawn Broth

Heat 2 tablespoons oil in a large saucepan and fry 2 sliced banana shallots and 2 sliced garlic cloves over a high heat, stirring, for 2–3 minutes. Reduce the heat, add 1 tablespoon korma curry paste and stir for 1 minute. Pour 1 litre (1¾ pints) hot vegetable stock into the pan. Add 300 g (10 oz) raw peeled king prawns, 250 g (8 oz) cooked long-grain rice, 2 seeded and diced tomatoes and 2 tablespoons chopped coriander. Simmer for 2–3 minutes, then ladle into bowls to serve.

20 Quick Prawn Curry

Heat 2 tablespoons oil in a large frying pan and cook 1 finely sliced onion, 2 sliced garlic cloves and 1 tablespoon peeled and chopped fresh root ginger over a medium-high heat for 3–4 minutes, until beginning to soften. Stir in 2 tablespoons korma curry paste and cook for 1 minute before adding a 400 g (13 oz) can chopped tomatoes and 200 ml (7 fl oz) water. Simmer for about 12 minutes, until thickened slightly, then add 500 g (1 lb) raw peeled king prawns. Simmer for a further 2–3 minutes, until the prawns are cooked. Serve with a dollop of natural yogurt and chopped coriander leaves.

Italian Beans with Pancetta

Serves 4

3 tablespoons extra virgin olive oil, plus extra to drizzle

300 g (10 oz) cubed pancetta

3 banana shallots, chopped

2 teaspoons chopped thyme

2 x 400 g (13 oz) cans borlotti beans, rinsed and drained

400 g (13 oz) can cannellini beans, rinsed and drained

200 ml (7 fl oz) vegetable stock

salt and pepper

To serve (optional)

crusty bread

Parmesan cheese, grated

parsley, freshly chopped

- Heat the oil in a heavy-based frying pan and fry the pancetta over a high heat for 2–3 minutes, until golden. Reduce the heat slightly, add the shallots and thyme and cook for a further 2–3 minutes, stirring occasionally, until just softened.

- Add the beans and vegetable stock, season with a pinch of salt and plenty of pepper and simmer over a medium heat for 2–3 minutes, until tender.

- Spoon into bowls, drizzle over a little extra olive oil and serve immediately with crusty bread, plenty of Parmesan and parsley, if desired.

 Italian Minestrone Soup with Pancetta Heat 2 tablespoons oil in a pan over a medium heat and cook 2 chopped shallots, 2 chopped garlic cloves, 1 chopped celery stick and 1 chopped carrot for 5–6 minutes, stirring. Add a 400 g (13 oz) can chopped tomatoes, a 400 g (13 oz) can rinsed and drained borlotti beans and 1 litre (1¾ pints) hot vegetable stock. Simmer for 10–12 minutes, adding 75 g (3 oz) mini pasta shapes for the final 5 minutes. Meanwhile, fry 200 g (7 oz) cubed pancetta over a medium-high heat for 5–6 minutes. Ladle the soup into bowls, sprinkle with the pancetta and serve as above.

Chunky Italian Stew with Pancetta Heat 2 tablespoons olive oil in a large saucepan or flameproof casserole dish over a medium-high heat and add 200 g (7 oz) cubed pancetta, 1 chopped onion, 2 chopped garlic cloves, 2 sliced celery sticks and 2 diced carrots. Cook for 5–6 minutes, until beginning to colour. Add 2 diced potatoes, a 400 g (13 oz) can roughly chopped plum tomatoes, a 400 g (13 oz) can rinsed and drained cannellini or borlotti beans, 1 teaspoon dried oregano and 750 ml (1¼ pints) hot vegetable or chicken stock. Season generously and simmer over a medium heat for about 15 minutes before adding 50 g (2 oz) macaroni or other small pasta. Cook for a further 5–6 minutes, until the pasta and vegetables are tender. Serve ladled into shallow bowls, as above.

 Spiced Tomato and Chorizo Soup

Serves 4

3 tablespoons olive oil
1 red onion, chopped
2 garlic cloves, chopped
1 teaspoon hot smoked paprika
2 x 400 g (13 oz) cans butter
  beans, chopped
100 g (3½ oz) sun-dried
  tomatoes, drained
500 g (1 lb) passata
900 ml (1½ pints) vegetable stock
150 g (5 oz) chorizo, diced
salt and pepper
chopped parsley, to garnish
crusty bread, to serve

- Heat 2 tablespoons of the oil in a large saucepan or flameproof casserole dish and cook the onion and garlic over a medium heat for 4–5 minutes, until slightly softened.

- Add the paprika and butter beans and stir for 1 minute before adding the sun-dried tomatoes, passata and stock. Bring to the boil, then simmer for about 10 minutes, until thickened slightly.

- Meanwhile, heat the remaining oil in a small frying pan and cook the chorizo for 2–3 minutes, stirring frequently, until golden. Drain on kitchen paper and set aside.

- Blend the soup to the desired consistency, then season to taste and ladle into bowls. Top with the chorizo and parsley and serve immediately with plenty of crusty bread.

 Spicy Tomato and Butter Bean Bowl

Heat 2 tablespoons oil in a frying pan over a medium heat and cook 200 g (7 oz) cubed chorizo sausage for 2–3 minutes. Reduce the heat slightly and add 1 chopped red chilli or 1 teaspoon dried chilli flakes and 1 chopped garlic clove. Fry for 1–2 minutes, until just softened. Add 2 x 400 g (13 oz) cans rinsed and drained butter beans and 4 diced ripe tomatoes. Stir gently for 2–3 minutes, until warmed through, then season. Add 2 tablespoons chopped flat leaf parsley and 2 teaspoons sherry vinegar, stir again and serve immediately with peppery rocket leaves, if desired.

 Spicy Tomato and Chorizo Casserole

Heat 1 tablespoon olive oil in a large saucepan or flameproof casserole dish over a medium heat. Cut a 225 g (7½ oz) spicy chorizo ring into chunks and cook for 2–3 minutes, stirring occasionally, until golden. Add 1 large sliced red onion and 2 chopped garlic cloves and cook for 4–5 minutes, to soften. Stir in 1 teaspoon hot smoked paprika, then add 500 g (1 lb) peeled and diced butternut squash and heat for 1 minute. Add 500 g (1 lb) passata, 150 ml (¼ pint) vegetable stock or water, 1 large drained and sliced roast pepper (optional) and a 400 g (13 oz) can rinsed and drained chickpeas or butter beans. Bring to the boil and season with salt and pepper, then cover and simmer for about 15 minutes, until the casserole is rich and thick and the squash is tender. Ladle into bowls and garnish with plenty of freshly chopped flat leaf parsley.

WIN-HEAR-HUY

30 Cowboy Beef and Bean Casserole

Serves 4

2 tablespoons olive oil
1 onion, chopped
2 garlic cloves, chopped
450 g (14½ oz) beef, in strips
1½ tablespoons chipotle paste
1 teaspoon ground cumin
1½ teaspoons sweet smoked
   paprika
175 g (6 oz) smoked pork
   sausage, thickly sliced
250 ml (8 fl oz) lager
400 g (13 oz) can chopped
   tomatoes
2 tablespoons tomato purée
400 g (13 oz) can beans (haricot,
   or kidney), rinsed and drained
1 roasted red pepper, drained
   and sliced (optional)
Tabasco or other hot sauce
salt and pepper

To serve

jacket potatoes or steamed rice
soured cream (optional)

- Heat the oil in a large saucepan or flameproof casserole dish. Add the onion and garlic and cook for 6–7 minutes, stirring frequently, to soften.

- Meanwhile, toss the beef strips in the chipotle paste, cumin and paprika. Add the beef and sausage to the onion mixture and stir over a medium heat for 1 minute. Add the lager, tomatoes, tomato purée, beans, red pepper (if using) and a few shakes of Tabasco. Season with salt and pepper, then cover and simmer over a medium-low heat for about 20 minutes, or until rich and thick.

- Ladle into dishes and serve with jacket potatoes or steamed rice, and a dollop of soured cream, if desired.

10 Cowboy Bean Stew

Heat 2 tablespoons oil in a frying pan over a medium-high heat. Mix 700 g (1 lb 7 oz) beef stir-fry strips with the chipotle paste and spices, as above, and stir-fry for 5–6 minutes, until the meat is browned. Add 2 x 400 g (13 oz) cans baked beans, heated, 1 tablespoon Worcestershire sauce and a few shakes of Tabasco. Serve as above.

20 Cowboy Beef and Bean Soup

Heat 2 tablespoons olive oil in a large saucepan or flameproof casserole dish and cook 1 finely chopped onion, 1 finely chopped celery stick and 1 chopped garlic clove over a medium heat for 3–4 minutes, until beginning to soften. Increase the heat and add 300 g (10 oz) lean minced beef, stirring frequently for 3–4 minutes, until browned all over. Add 2 tablespoons tomato purée and stir constantly for 1 minute. Pour in 1 litre (1¾ pints) hot beef stock plus a 400 g (13 oz) can rinsed and drained pinto or black beans and a few shakes of Tabasco. Simmer over a medium heat for about 10 minutes to allow the flavours to develop. Ladle into bowls and serve immediately.

WIN-HEAR-PEG

Soupy Butternut Squash and Ham Rice Bowl

Serves 4

800 g (1 lb 10 oz) peeled
  butternut squash, cut into 1 cm
  (½ inch) cubes
2 tablespoons sweet chilli sauce
2 spring onions, finely sliced
2 teaspoons peeled and chopped
  fresh root ginger
1.2 litres (2 pints) good-quality,
  boiling ham or vegetable stock
200 g (7 oz) piece cooked ham,
  shredded or diced
250 g (8 oz) cooked rice
salt and pepper
chopped coriander, to garnish
  (optional)

- Place the squash, chilli sauce, spring onions and ginger in a large saucepan, add the stock and cook for about 8 minutes, until the squash is just tender.

- Add the ham and rice to the pan for the final 2 minutes. Season to taste and ladle into bowls and serve garnished with the coriander, if desired.

20 Ham and Butternut Squash Soup

Place 2 tablespoons olive oil in a large saucepan over a medium-low heat and cook 2 teaspoons peeled and finely chopped fresh root ginger, ½–1 teaspoon chilli flakes (depending on heat desired) and 2 chopped garlic cloves for about 2 minutes, until softened. Add 900 g (1 lb 13 oz) peeled and diced butternut squash and 1.2 litres (2 pints) hot vegetable stock and simmer for 12–15 minutes, until the squash is tender. Add 250 g (8 oz) diced cooked ham and blend the soup to the desired consistency. Ladle into bowls to serve.

30 Torn Ham and Butternut Squash

Casserole Place 2 tablespoons olive oil in a large saucepan or flameproof casserole dish over a medium heat and cook 1 sliced red onion for 5–6 minutes, until beginning to soften. Add 2 chopped garlic cloves, 2 teaspoons peeled and chopped fresh root ginger, ½–1 teaspoon chilli flakes (depending on heat desired) and 1 teaspoon cumin seeds. Cook for a further 2 minutes, then add 900 g (1 lb 13 oz) peeled chunks of butternut squash. Add 500 ml (17 fl oz) vegetable stock and half a cinnamon stick, and simmer for 12–15 minutes, until thick and tender. Stir 250 g (8 oz) ready-cooked mixed grains or pearl barley into the casserole along with 250 g (8 oz) torn cooked ham. Bring back to a simmer, season with pepper and serve ladled into dishes.

30 White Bean, Bacon and Cabbage Soup with Rosemary Pistou

Serves 4

4 tablespoons olive oil

200 g (7 oz) thick-cut bacon, chopped

1 onion, chopped

1 celery stick, sliced

1 carrot, diced

1 litre (1¾ pints) ham stock

1 bay leaf

400 g (13 oz) can cannellini or haricot beans, rinsed and drained

2 tablespoons chopped rosemary

1 small garlic clove, crushed

½ small head of Savoy cabbage, shredded (about 250 g/8 oz prepared weight)

salt and pepper

Parmesan cheese, grated, to serve

- Heat 1 tablespoon of the oil in a large saucepan or flameproof casserole dish and cook the bacon for 2–3 minutes over a medium-high heat to brown. Add the onion, celery and carrot, reduce the heat slightly, and cook for 5–6 minutes, stirring occasionally, until slightly softened.

- Add the stock and bay leaf and bring to the boil. Add the beans and simmer for 10–12 minutes, until the vegetables are almost tender.

- Meanwhile, using a small food processor or a pestle and mortar, grind the rosemary with the remaining 3 tablespoons oil, the garlic and a pinch of salt and pepper.

- Add the cabbage to the soup and simmer for a further 3–5 minutes, until just tender. Season to taste, then ladle into bowls and serve hot, drizzled with a little rosemary pistou and a sprinkling of Parmesan.

---

10 Wilted Winter Greens with Bacon and Pesto

Heat 2 tablespoons oil in a large saucepan and cook 200 g (7 oz) chopped bacon for about 3–4 minutes, until golden. Add 2 crushed garlic cloves, cook for 1 minute, then pour in 500 ml (17 fl oz) hot ham stock and 2 tablespoons pesto. Return to the boil, then stir in 400 g (13 oz) shredded winter greens (such as kale, chard, Savoy cabbage, spinach) or spring greens. Simmer for 3–4 minutes, until just tender, then ladle into bowls and serve with extra pesto, if desired.

20 Winter Greens Soup with Pistou

Melt 25 g (1 oz) butter with 2 tablespoons olive oil in a large saucepan and cook 1 chopped onion, 1 chopped potato and 2 thinly sliced leeks over a medium heat for 5–6 minutes, until beginning to soften. Meanwhile, prepare the pistou sauce as in the main recipe. Pour 1 litre (1¾ pints) boiling vegetable or ham stock into the onion mixture, then cover and simmer for 7–8 minutes, until the vegetables are almost tender. Add 250 g (8 oz) shredded winter greens or spring greens and cook for 3–4 minutes, until everything is tender. Blend the soup to desired consistency, then ladle into bowls and serve drizzled with the pistou, as above.

WIN-HEAR-HAY

10 Thai Chicken Noodle Broth

Serves 4

1 tablespoon vegetable oil
2 tablespoons green Thai
  curry paste
1 litre (1¾ pints) good-quality
  clear chicken stock
1 tablespoon fish sauce
1 teaspoon sugar
1 sliced red chilli (optional)
2–3 kaffir lime leaves, shredded
  (optional)
250 g (8 oz) thin rice noodles
250 g (8 oz) cooked chicken,
  shredded
thinly sliced spring onions,
  to garnish (optional)

- Heat the oil in a large saucepan and cook the curry paste for 1 minute over a medium-low heat, until aromatic. Pour in the chicken stock, then add the fish sauce, sugar, chilli and lime leaves, if using. Bring to the boil and simmer for 4–5 minutes to allow the flavours to develop.

- Meanwhile, bring a large pan of water to the boil. Add the noodles, then turn off the heat and set aside for 3 minutes, until tender. Alternatively, cook according to the packet instructions. Drain well, then divide the noodles between 4 bowls. Top with the shredded chicken, then ladle over the hot broth. Garnish with spring onions to serve, if desired.

 Winter Thai Chicken Soup

Heat 2 tablespoons oil in a large saucepan and cook 2 sliced banana shallots for 2–3 minutes, until beginning to soften. Add 600 g (1 lb 3½ oz) mixed chopped sweet potato and butternut squash and 2 tablespoons Thai red curry paste. Cook for 1 minute over a medium-low heat, then pour in 600 ml (1 pint) hot chicken stock and 400 ml (14 fl oz) coconut milk with the fish sauce, sugar, chilli and lime leaves from the main recipe. Simmer for 12–15 minutes, until tender. Stir in 250 g (8 oz) cooked, shredded chicken, then ladle the soup into bowls to serve.

 Winter Thai Chicken Curry

Heat 2 tablespoons vegetable oil in a large saucepan and cook 2 sliced banana shallots for 2–3 minutes, until beginning to soften. Add 500 g (1 lb) boned, skinless chicken thighs to the pan and cook for 3–4 minutes, stirring occasionally, until the meat changes colour. Stir in a 600 g (1 lb 3½ oz) mixture of diced winter vegetables, such as butternut squash, celeriac, parsnip and sweet potato. Add 2 tablespoons green Thai curry paste and stir for 1–2 minutes, until the chicken and vegetables are coated and aromatic. Pour in 400 ml (14 fl oz) coconut milk and 200 ml (7 fl oz) chicken stock, plus the fish sauce, sugar, red chilli and lime leaves from the main recipe. Simmer gently for about 15 minutes, until the vegetables are tender. Serve with steamed Thai rice.

10 Quick Sausage and Mushroom Stew

Serves 4

2 tablespoons olive oil
2 garlic cloves, sliced
2 spring onions, sliced
250 g (8 oz) chestnut
  mushrooms, halved
700 g (1 lb 7 oz) tomato pasta
  sauce
200 g (7 oz) cocktail-sized
  cooked sausages, halved

To serve

Parmesan cheese, grated
Crusty bread

- Heat the olive oil in a deep-sided frying pan and cook the garlic and spring onions over a medium heat for 1 minute, until slightly softened. Add the mushrooms and cook for about 5 minutes, stirring occasionally, until soft and golden.

- Add the pasta sauce and sausages and stir over the heat for 2–3 minutes, until hot. Serve immediately with plenty of crusty bread and grated Parmesan.

---

20 Cumberland Sausage Hotpot with Mushrooms

Grill 8 Cumberland-style sausages under a preheated medium-hot grill for 12 minutes, turning occasionally, until cooked through. Meanwhile, heat 2 tablespoons oil in a saucepan, add 1 sliced onion and 2 chopped garlic cloves and cook for 4–5 minutes. Add 250 g (8 oz) halved mushrooms and cook for a further 4–5 minutes. Pour in 700 g (1 lb 7 oz) tomato-based pasta sauce and simmer for 2–3 minutes. Once the sausages are cool enough to handle, slice diagonally and add to the pan. Cook, stirring, for a further 2 minutes, then serve with crispy fried potatoes and freshly grated Parmesan.

30 Farmhouse Sausage and Mushroom Crumble

Grill the sausages and prepare the mushroom stew following the 20-minute recipe, then place the sausages in a shallow ovenproof dish. Meanwhile, put 75 g (3 oz) freshly made coarse breadcrumbs in a bowl and stir in 2 tablespoons olive oil, 2 finely chopped spring onions, 2 tablespoons freshly grated Parmesan, 1 tablespoon finely chopped mixed herbs (such as parsley, rosemary and thyme) and a pinch of salt and pepper. Cover the sausages with the mushroom stew and stir lightly to combine. Scatter the crumble mixture evenly over the top and place in a preheated oven, 200°C (400°F), Gas Mark 6, for 12–15 minutes, until crisp and lightly golden. Serve with a green salad.

WIN-HEAR-DAP

10 Hearty Pea and Lentil Soup with Crispy Cured Ham

Serves 4

50 g (2 oz) butter
3 spring onions, sliced
1 garlic clove, crushed
600 ml (1 pint) hot ham or
   vegetable stock
400 g (13 oz) can chickpeas,
   rinsed and drained
400 g (13 oz) can green lentils
   in water, rinsed and drained
200 g (7 oz) frozen peas
3 sage leaves, chopped (optional)
1 tablespoon olive oil
4 slices of Black Forest or
   Parma ham
salt and pepper

- Melt the butter in a large saucepan and cook the spring onions and garlic over a medium heat for 1–2 minutes, until softened.

- Add the stock, chickpeas, lentils, peas and sage, if using. Simmer for 5–6 minutes, until the peas are tender.

- Meanwhile, heat the oil in a large frying pan and fry the ham until crispy, turning once. Drain on kitchen paper.

- Blend the soup to the desired consistency, season to taste then ladle into bowls and crumble some of the ham on top.

 Ham and Lentil 'Peasouper'

Melt 50 g (2 oz) butter in a large saucepan and add 1 chopped onion, 1 chopped celery stick, 2 chopped garlic cloves and 2 chopped potatoes. Cook over a medium-low heat for 10 minutes, stirring frequently, until softened. Add 1.2 litres (2 pints) hot ham stock, a 400 g (13 oz) can drained green lentils, 250 g (8 oz) piece of chopped ham and 200 g (7 oz) frozen peas. Bring to the boil and simmer for 5–6 minutes, until the peas are soft. Blend to the desired consistency, then ladle into bowls and serve garnished with crumbled crispy bacon.

 Chunky Ham and Lentil Stew

Melt 50 g (2 oz) butter in a large casserole and add 2 thickly sliced leeks, 1 sliced celery stick, 2 diced carrots, 1 chopped onion, 2 chopped garlic cloves and 2 chunkily chopped potatoes. Cook over a medium-low heat for 12–15 minutes, until softened and lightly coloured. Add 500 g (1 lb) ready-cooked Puy lentils and 350 g (11½ oz) cooked, pulled ham hock (if unavailable, cut or tear the meat from a piece of ham into bite-sized pieces). Pour in 500 ml (17 fl oz) hot ham or vegetable stock, add 2 thyme sprigs and 1 bay leaf and simmer over a medium heat for about 10 minutes, until the vegetables are tender. Serve ladled into bowls with freshly cooked peas and crusty bread.

Mexican Beef Chilli Soup

Serves 4

2 tablespoons vegetable oil
1 large red pepper, cut into strips
1 red onion, halved and thinly sliced
1 red chilli, thinly sliced
1½ teaspoons ground cumin
2 tablespoons tomato purée
1 litre (1¾ pints) hot beef stock
400 g (13 oz) can black beans or
  kidney beans, rinsed and drained
125 g (4 oz) frozen or canned
  sweetcorn, drained if necessary
300 g (10 oz) thick beef steak
2 tablespoons lime juice
coriander leaves, to garnish

To serve (optional)
tortilla chips
grated cheese

- Heat 1 tablespoon of the oil in a large saucepan and cook the pepper and onion over a medium-high heat for 4–5 minutes, until lightly coloured. Reduce the heat, add the chilli, cumin and tomato purée and stir for 1 minute.

- Add the stock, beans and sweetcorn, then simmer for 5–6 minutes, to allow the flavours to develop.

- Meanwhile, heat the remaining tablespoon oil in a frying pan and cook the steak for 1–2 minutes each side, depending on pinkness desired. Transfer to a plate and leave to rest for 2–3 minutes. Slice the steak into strips, cutting against the grain, and pour any juices from it into the soup.

- Ladle the soup into bowls, add the beef and lime juice, garnish with coriander and serve immediately, accompanied by tortilla chips and grated cheese, if desired.

Mexican Pepper and Meatball Bowl

Heat 2 tablespoons oil in a pan and cook 1 sliced red pepper and 1 sliced red onion over a medium-high heat for 5–6 minutes. Reduce the heat, then add 350 g (11½ oz) cooked meatballs plus 2 teaspoons Mexican spice blend and stir for 1 minute. Pour in 500 g (1 lb) Mexican cooking sauce and bring to the boil. Simmer for 1–2 minutes. Spoon into bowls, garnish with coriander and serve immediately with tortilla chips and grated cheese, or with steamed rice for a meal.

Mexican Meatball Stew

Heat 2 tablespoons vegetable oil in a large, deep-sided frying pan and add 500 g (1 lb) shop-bought meatballs. Alternatively, remove the casings from 8 spicy sausages and form into 20–24 meatballs. Cook over a medium-high heat, shaking the pan frequently, for 6–7 minutes, until the meatballs are browned all over. Transfer to a plate and set aside. Add 1 sliced red pepper, 1 sliced yellow pepper and 1 sliced red onion, and cook over a high heat for 3–4 minutes, until lightly charred. Reduce the heat slightly, add 1 tablespoon Mexican-style spice blend and stir for 1 minute. Return the meatballs to the pan with a 680 g (1 lb 6 oz) jar passata, a 400 g (13 oz) can rinsed and drained kidney beans and 125 g (4 oz) canned or frozen sweetcorn (optional). Simmer over a medium heat for about 15 minutes, until the meatballs are cooked and the sauce is rich and thick. Serve in bowls, garnished with coriander leaves and accompanied by cooked rice, soured cream and grated cheese.

QuickCook

Winter
Cold-
Busters

Recipes listed by cooking time

3

2

10

10 Smoked Salmon and Edamame Cups

Serves 4

250 g (8 oz) edamame beans

200 g (7 oz) smoked salmon, thinly sliced

¼ cucumber, deseeded and cut into matchsticks

1 red chilli, deseeded and sliced

2 tablespoons sweet soy sauce

2 tablespoons roughly chopped coriander leaves (optional)

3–4 little gem lettuces

2 teaspoons sesame seeds

- Cook the beans in a large pan of salted, boiling water for 1–2 minutes, or according to the packet instructions, until just tender. Drain and cool under cold running water.

- Meanwhile, combine the salmon, cucumber, chilli, soy sauce and coriander in a bowl. Add the beans and toss gently to combine. Separate the lettuce leaves.

- Spoon the bean mixture into the lettuce leaves and scatter the sesame seeds over the top. Serve immediately.

20 Seared Salmon with Quinoa, Lentil and Edamame Salad

Rub 2 tablespoons teriyaki sauce over 4 boneless salmon fillets. Heat 1 tablespoon groundnut oil in a nonstick frying pan and sear the salmon over a medium–high heat for 2–3 minutes on each side. Transfer to a plate, cover with foil and set aside to rest. Meanwhile, cook 250 g (8 oz) edamame beans as in the main recipe. Place 250 g (8 oz) each of cooked Puy lentils, cooked red quinoa and cooked white quinoa in a bowl. Add a quarter of a deseeded and diced cucumber, 1 deseeded and finely chopped red chilli, 2 finely sliced spring onions and 2 tablespoons chopped coriander. Make a dressing by combining 2 tablespoons sweet soy sauce with 3 tablespoons lime juice and 1 tablespoon sesame oil. Stir half into the quinoa mixture along with the cooled soya beans, then divide the salad between 4 serving dishes. Top with the seared salmon fillets, sprinkle with 1 teaspoon sesame seeds and drizzle with the remaining dressing, if desired.

30 Roasted Salmon with Quinoa and Edamame Beans

Combine 4 tablespoons teriyaki marinade with 1 tablespoon sesame oil and rub over 4 boneless salmon fillets. Marinate in a small roasting tin for 10 minutes. Bring 400 ml (14 fl oz) vegetable stock to the boil in a pan, add 200 g (7 oz) quinoa and cook for 12–15 minutes. Drain. Meanwhile, sprinkle 2 teaspoons sesame seeds over the salmon fillets and place in a preheated oven, 200°C (400°F), Gas Mark 6, for 12–15 minutes, until just cooked through. Cook 250 g (8 oz) edamame beans as in the main recipe and stir them into the quinoa. Heap on to plates, top with the salmon and serve with cucumber ribbons and dressing from the 20-minute recipe.

1⃝ Crunchy Beef Wraps

Serves 2

1 tablespoon vegetable oil
1 sirloin steak, about 200 g (7 oz)
3 tablespoons crunchy peanut
  butter
1 red chilli, deseeded and chopped
1 tablespoon dark soy sauce
1 teaspoon finely grated lime rind
150 g (5 oz) mixture of bean
  sprouts, mangetout and carrot
2 large, soft plain tortilla wraps
1 tablespoon chopped coriander
2 teaspoons lime juice
salt and pepper

- Heat the oil in a frying pan over a high heat and cook the steak for 2–3 minutes on each side, until nicely browned but still medium-rare. Transfer to a plate and set aside to rest.

- Meanwhile, put the peanut butter in a small bowl, add the chilli, soy sauce and lime rind and whisk well.

- Shred the mangetout and cut the carrot into batons.

- Spread the peanut butter mixture over the tortillas, then top with the mixed vegetables and coriander.

- Slice the steak thinly against the grain and arrange it over the vegetables. Drizzle with the lime juice, season with a pinch of salt and pepper, then roll up tightly to serve.

2⃝ Sizzling Beef and Mangetout

Stir-Fry Heat 1 tablespoon oil in a wok and cook 200 g (7 oz) thinly sliced beef sirloin over a high heat for 2–3 minutes. Transfer the meat to a plate and set aside. Add another tablespoon of oil to the wok and stir-fry 1 sliced garlic clove, 2 teaspoons peeled and chopped fresh root ginger, 1 chopped red chilli, 150 g (5 oz) shredded mangetout and 1 sliced red pepper over a high heat for 3–4 minutes. Return the beef to the pan with a handful of bean sprouts and toss for a further minute. Add 2 tablespoons soy sauce, 2 teaspoons sesame oil and 1 tablespoon lime juice and cook for a final minute. Serve with rice and sprinkle with crushed peanuts.

3⃝ Marinated Beef Skewers with

Mangetout Noodles Slice 250 g (8 oz) thick beef sirloin into long, thin strips. Place in a dish with 1 tablespoon soy sauce, 1 teaspoon finely grated lime rind and 2 teaspoons sesame oil. Mix well. Set aside to marinate for 10 minutes, then thread on to 4 metal skewers. Place 1 tablespoon oil in a large frying pan and cook the beef skewers over a medium-high heat for 4–5 minutes, turning occasionally, until just cooked. Transfer to a plate, cover with foil and keep warm. Meanwhile, return the pan to the heat and stir-fry the garlic, ginger, chilli, mangetout and red pepper following the 10-minute recipe.

Add 300 g (10 oz) straight-to-wok-style rice noodles plus 1 tablespoon light soy sauce, 1 teaspoon sesame oil and 1 tablespoon lime juice. Toss well and heat until hot. Heap into serving dishes, top with the beef skewers and their juices and scatter with chopped coriander and crushed peanuts to serve.

30 Feed-a-Cold Chicken Soup

Serves 4

1.2 litres (2 pints) hot chicken or
  vegetable stock

1 bay leaf

500 g (1 lb) boneless, skinless
  chicken thighs, trimmed of fat

25 g (1 oz) butter

1 celery stick, thinly sliced

2 leeks, thinly sliced

2 carrots, thinly sliced

125 g (4 oz) mushrooms, sliced

1 garlic clove, chopped

75 g (3 oz) frozen sweetcorn

75 g (3 oz) angel hair pasta

salt and pepper

chilli oil, to drizzle (optional)

chopped parsley, to garnish

- Bring the stock and bay leaf to the boil in a saucepan and add the chicken. Cover loosely and simmer for 20 minutes, until cooked and tender. Scoop out the meat with a slotted spoon and set aside to cool slightly, reserving the stock.

- Meanwhile, melt the butter in a large pan and cook the celery, leeks and carrots for 7–8 minutes, until softened. Add the mushrooms and garlic and cook for further 3–4 minutes.

- Pour in the reserved stock, add the corn and return to the boil. Season to taste. Tip the pasta into the pan and cook for 3–4 minutes, or until 'al dente'.

- Shred the chicken and add to the broth. Ladle into deep bowls and serve drizzled with chilli oil, if desired, and garnished with chopped parsley and freshly ground black pepper.

 Instant Goodness Chicken Noodle Broth Heat 1 litre (1¾ pints) chicken stock in a large pan with 2 teaspoons peeled and chopped fresh root ginger, 1 sliced garlic clove, 1 deseeded and sliced red chilli, 75 g (3 oz) sweetcorn, 125 g (4 oz) sliced chestnut mushrooms and 1 tablespoon soy sauce. Simmer for 7–8 minutes, then add 250 g (8 oz) shredded cooked chicken breast. Meanwhile, cook 200 g (7 oz) medium egg noodles according to the packet instructions. Heap into 4 bowls, ladle the broth over them and serve immediately, garnished with thinly sliced spring onions.

 Quick Creamy Chicken and Corn Chowder Melt 50 g (2 oz) butter in a large pan over a medium heat and cook 2 chopped leeks, 1 sliced celery stick and 1 chopped garlic clove for 3–4 minutes, until beginning to soften. Pour 1 litre (1¾ pints) milk into a separate pan with 1 teaspoon chopped thyme, 2 cloves and 1 bay leaf and heat to boiling point. Meanwhile, add 400 g (13 oz) finely diced potatoes to the vegetables with 200 g (7 oz) diced mushrooms. Sprinkle in 1 tablespoon plain flour, then season generously and stir over the heat for 1 minute. Stir the hot infused milk into the pan and simmer for 8–10 minutes, until the potato is almost tender. Add 350 g (11½ oz) diced chicken breast and 150 g (5 oz) sweetcorn and simmer for 2–3 minutes, until the chicken is cooked. Stir 75 g (3 oz) grated mature Cheddar cheese (optional) into the chowder, then season to taste and serve ladled into bowls with lots of crusty bread.

WIN-WINT-TUH

Smoked Mackerel Salad with Orange and Avocado

Serves 4

4 peppered smoked mackerel fillets, skin removed
2 small oranges
2 tablespoons avocado oil
175 g (6 oz) rocket and watercress salad
2 firm avocados, peeled, stoned and sliced
50 g (2 oz) walnut halves (optional)
salt and pepper

- Flake the smoked mackerel fillets.

- Using a sharp knife, cut the top and bottom off each orange. Slice away the skin and pith, then cut into segments, slicing either side of the membrane. Squeeze out the membrane before discarding it, then pour all the juice into a bowl.

- Place 3 tablespoons of the reserved juice in another bowl, add the avocado oil, salt and pepper and whisk together.

- Combine the salad leaves gently with the flaked mackerel, orange segments and avocado, and arrange attractively on serving plates. Scatter over the walnuts, if using, then drizzle over the dressing to serve.

---

2 **Grilled Mackerel with Orange and Avocado Salsa** Rub 1 tablespoon olive oil over 8 small, boneless mackerel fillets, then season with salt and pepper. Arrange skin-side up on a foil-lined grill rack and slide under a preheated medium-hot grill for 4–5 minutes. Turn carefully and cook for a further 1–2 minutes, until the flesh turns white. Remove from the heat, cover loosely with foil and set aside to rest. Meanwhile, cut 2 small oranges into segments, following the instructions in the main recipe and reserving the juice. Dice the flesh neatly and place in a bowl with 2 small peeled, stoned and diced avocados. Drizzle over 2 tablespoons avocado oil, 2 tablespoons of the orange juice and 1 teaspoon red wine vinegar. Add 1 teaspoon chopped dill, season to taste, then toss gently and serve with the grilled mackerel fillets and a rocket and watercress salad.

3  **Orangey Marinated Mackerel with Avocado** Place 1 teaspoon grated orange rind in a bowl with 1 tablespoon orange juice, 2 tablespoons avocado oil, 1 tablespoon wholegrain mustard, 1 teaspoon runny honey, 2 tablespoons chopped parsley and 1 teaspoon chopped dill. Season and mix well. Cut 3–4 slits in each side of 4 whole scaled, gutted and cleaned mackerel and place the fish side by side in an ovenproof dish. Cover with the prepared marinade, massaging it into the slits, and place in a preheated oven, 200°C (400°F), Gas Mark 6, for 20–22 minutes. Serve with steamed new potatoes and an avocado and rocket salad.

Grilled Lamb with Kale and Spicy Tomato Salsa

Serves 4

1 teaspoon dried oregano
2 tablespoons olive oil
1 teaspoon grated lemon rind
4 lamb steaks
250 g (8 oz) curly kale leaves,
    roughly sliced
salt and pepper

For the salsa

300 g (10 oz) ripe tomatoes,
    deseeded and diced
½ small red onion, finely chopped
1 large red chilli, finely chopped
pinch of sugar
2 teaspoons lemon juice
1 tablespoon olive oil
2 tablespoons chopped parsley

- Combine the oregano, olive oil and lemon rind in a bowl with a pinch of salt and pepper, and rub the mixture all over the lamb steaks. Arrange on a foil-lined grill rack and slide under a preheated hot grill for 6–8 minutes, turning once, until cooked to your liking.

- Meanwhile, cook the kale in a large pan of salted boiling water for 5–6 minutes, until tender.

- Combine the salsa ingredients in a bowl and season to taste.

- Heap the kale on to serving plates, then arrange the lamb on top and serve with the salsa.

 Spiced Lamb and Tomato Skewers Place 400 g (13 oz) diced lamb in a large bowl with ½–1 teaspoon crushed chilli flakes plus the oregano, olive oil, lemon rind and seasoning from the main recipe. Add 250 g (8 oz) red and yellow cherry tomatoes and 1 red onion cut into bite-sized pieces. Mix to coat, then thread on to 4 metal skewers and arrange on a foil-lined grill rack. Slide under a preheated medium-hot grill for 8–12 minutes, turning occasionally. Arrange on serving plates with the kale and salsa from the main recipe.

Spicy Lamb and Tomato Orecchiette Heat 2 tablespoons oil in a large frying pan and cook 1 chopped onion, 2 chopped garlic cloves and 1 deseeded and chopped red chilli over a medium heat for 6–7 minutes, stirring frequently, until softened. Increase the heat slightly and add 400 g (13 oz) minced lamb and cook for 3–4 minutes, stirring occasionally, until browned. Pour in 500 g (1 lb) passata, then add 1 tablespoon tomato purée, 1 teaspoon finely grated lemon rind, 1 teaspoon dried oregano, a pinch of sugar and a generous pinch of salt and pepper. Bring to the boil, then simmer, loosely covered, for about 15 minutes, adding 100 g (3½ oz) shredded kale for the final 7–8 minutes. Meanwhile, cook 400 g (13 oz) orecchiette pasta in a large pan of salted boiling water for about 10 minutes, or according to the packet instructions, until 'al dente'. Drain and serve with the spicy lamb, garnished with chopped oregano or parsley, if desired.

2 ⏱ Crispy Salmon Ramen

Serves 2

2 teaspoons groundnut oil

2 boneless salmon fillets, skin on

500 ml (17 fl oz) hot clear chicken stock

1 tablespoon lime juice

2 teaspoons fish sauce

1 tablespoon soy sauce

1.5 cm (¾ inch) piece of fresh root ginger, peeled and cut into matchsticks

1 small red chilli, thinly sliced

2 heads of pak choi, sliced in half lengthways

150 g (5 oz) ramen or egg noodles

coriander leaves, to garnish

- Place the oil in a large frying pan over a medium heat and fry the salmon fillets, skin-side down, for 3–5 minutes, until the skin is really crispy. Turn carefully and cook for a further minute, until still slightly rare. Transfer to a plate and keep warm.

- Pour the stock into a saucepan, add the lime juice, fish sauce, soy sauce and ginger and bring to the boil. Simmer for 3–4 minutes, then add the chilli and pak choi and simmer for another 4–5 minutes, until tender.

- Meanwhile, cook the noodles in a pan of boiling water for 2–3 minutes, or according to the packet instructions, until just tender. Drain and heap into bowls.

- Ladle over the hot broth and top each bowl with a salmon fillet. Serve immediately, garnished with coriander leaves.

---

1 ⏱ Crispy Salmon with Noodles

Cook the salmon fillets following the main recipe. Meanwhile, heat 250 g (8 oz) ready-to-use egg noodles following the packet instructions. Place 1 tablespoon vegetable oil in a large wok or frying pan over a medium-high heat. Add 2 chopped garlic cloves, 2 teaspoons peeled and chopped fresh root ginger, 2 sliced spring onions and 1 thinly sliced red chilli. Stir-fry for 2–3 minutes, then add a large handful of bean sprouts for a further 1–2 minutes, until softened slightly. Add the noodles plus 1 tablespoon lime juice, 1 tablespoon soy sauce and 1 teaspoon sesame seeds. Heap the noodle mixture into bowls, top with the salmon and serve immediately, garnished with coriander.

3 ⏱ Steamed Salmon with Chilli and Ginger

Arrange 2 boneless salmon fillets on a large piece of foil and top with the lime juice, fish sauce, soy sauce, ginger and chilli from the main recipe. Fold up the sides of the foil and scrunch together to enclose the fish. Place in a steamer over a pan of barely simmering water for about 12 minutes, or until the salmon is aromatic and almost cooked. Serve with steamed pak choi and rice, garnished with sesame seeds and coriander.

30 Roasted Sprouts Chinese-Style

Serves 2

300 g (10 oz) Brussels sprouts
1 tablespoon vegetable oil
1 garlic clove, crushed
2 teaspoons peeled and finely
grated fresh root ginger
2 tablespoons light soy sauce
1 teaspoon sesame oil
1½ tablespoons runny honey
2 tablespoons orange juice
1 star anise
large handful of bean sprouts
toasted sesame seeds, to garnish

- Trim the sprouts, cut any large ones in half through the stem, then tip them into a roasting tin and toss with the oil. Roast in a preheated oven, 200°C (400°F), Gas Mark 6, for 20–25 minutes, until softened and browned. Meanwhile, combine the garlic, ginger, soy sauce, sesame oil, honey, orange juice and star anise in a small pan and place over a medium-low heat. Simmer for 4–5 minutes, stirring occasionally. Set aside and keep warm.

- Transfer the Brussels sprouts to a serving dish, add the bean sprouts and warm sauce and toss together. Serve sprinkled with toasted sesame seeds.

10 Shredded Sprout and Cabbage Salad with Ginger Dressing

Soak 200 g (7 oz) chilled, thin rice noodles in boiling water to soften. Slice 200 g (7 oz) trimmed Brussels sprouts. Thinly shred ¼ head Chinese cabbage. Place 2 tablespoons oil in a frying pan and stir-fry the sprouts and cabbage over a medium-high heat for 3–4 minutes. Meanwhile, whisk together 1 teaspoon peeled and grated fresh root ginger with 1 tablespoon orange juice, 2 teaspoons runny honey, 2 tablespoons soy sauce and 2 teaspoons sesame oil. Drain the noodles, then toss with the sprouts and cabbage, 2 teaspoons toasted sesame seeds and the dressing. Heap into bowls and serve immediately.

20 Chinese-Style Sprout and Ginger Stir-Fry

Place 2 tablespoons soy sauce in a bowl with 3 tablespoons freshly squeezed orange juice, 2 teaspoons sesame oil and 1 teaspoon Chinese five spice powder. Cut 250 g (8 oz) trimmed Brussels sprouts into quarters, through the stem. Place 1 tablespoon vegetable oil in a large wok or frying pan over a medium-high heat, add 2 sliced garlic cloves, a 2.5 cm (1 inch) piece of peeled and finely shredded fresh root ginger, and 1 deseeded and sliced red chilli. Stir-fry for 30 seconds, then add the sprouts and stir-fry for 3–4 minutes, until beginning to brown. Stir in ¼ head finely shredded Chinese cabbage and cook for 2 minutes, until softened but still with some 'bite'. Reduce the heat to low, then add the prepared sauce, stirring well. Heap the mixture into bowls and serve with steamed rice sprinkled with toasted sesame seeds.

 Poached Smoked Haddock
with Fried Eggs

Serves 4

600 ml (1 pint) milk
1 bay leaf
small thyme sprig
pinch of salt
¼ teaspoon cracked mixed
   peppercorns, plus extra to serve
4 smoked haddock fillets
2 tablespoons olive oil
4 eggs
1 kg (2 lb) ready-cooked chilled
   colcannon or mashed potato

- Pour the milk into a deep-sided frying pan. Add the bay, thyme, salt and peppercorns and bring to simmering point.

- Add the haddock fillets and simmer very gently for about 5–6 minutes, until the flesh turns opaque.

- Meanwhile, heat the oil in a large frying pan and fry the eggs for about 3 minutes, or until cooked to your liking.

- Heat the colcannon or mashed potato according to the packet instructions and spoon on to 4 plates. Top with the poached haddock, fried eggs and black pepper to serve.

 Pan-Fried Haddock Fillet with Mashed Potatoes and Poached Egg

Cook 700 g (1 lb 7 oz) diced floury potatoes in a pan of salted boiling water for 12–15 minutes. Dust 4 boneless haddock fillets with seasoned flour, shaking off the excess. Heat 2 tablespoons oil in a frying pan and cook the fish for 6–8 minutes, turning once. Meanwhile, bring a pan of water to a simmer. Stir the water to create a whirlpool and break an egg into the middle of it. Poach for 3 minutes, then remove with a slotted spoon and drain on kitchen paper. Poach 3 more eggs in the same way. Drain the potatoes and return to the pan with 50 g (2 oz) butter, 3 tablespoons milk and salt and pepper. Mash until smooth, then serve with the haddock and eggs.

Roasted Haddock with Crispy Potatoes and Poached Eggs

Halve 500 g (1 lb) baby new potatoes. Place in a roasting tin and add 1½ tablespoons olive oil, 1 teaspoon dried thyme, 2 unpeeled garlic cloves and a generous pinch of salt and pepper. Toss well, then roast in a preheated oven, 220°C (425°F), Gas Mark 7, for 20–25 minutes, turning occasionally, until the potatoes are crisp and tender. Meanwhile, heat 1 tablespoon olive oil in a large, flameproof frying pan. Add 4 pieces chunky haddock fillet and fry over a medium-high heat, skin-side down, for 2–3 minutes, until the skin is crispy. Drizzle with ½ tablespoon olive oil, season with coarsely ground mixed peppercorns and a small pinch of salt and transfer the pan to the oven for 8–10 minutes, until the fish is just cooked and flaky. Meanwhile, poach the eggs as in the 20-minute recipe. Serve with the crispy potatoes and roasted haddock.

3⟐ Roasted Squash and Chickpea Tagine

Serves 4

450 g (14½ oz) peeled butternut
   squash, cut into chunks
3 tablespoons olive oil
1 red onion, cut into thin wedges
2 garlic cloves, chopped
1.5 cm (¾ inch) root ginger, chopped
2 teaspoons ras el hanout
1 courgette, cut into chunks
400 g (13 oz) can chickpeas
400 g (13 oz) can chopped
   tomatoes
2 teaspoons honey
125 ml (4 fl oz) vegetable stock
salt and pepper

To garnish
chopped coriander
toasted flaked almonds

- Put the squash into a roasting tin, add 1 tablespoon of the olive oil and season generously with salt and pepper. Toss well, then roast in a preheated oven, 220°C (425°F), Gas Mark 7, for 20–25 minutes, turning occasionally, until tender.

- Meanwhile, heat the remaining oil in a large, flameproof casserole dish and fry the onion, garlic and ginger over a medium heat for 5–6 minutes. Stir in the ras el hanout and courgette, cook for 1 minute, then add the chickpeas, tomatoes, honey and stock. Stir to combine and simmer gently for 15–18 minutes, until thickened and tender.

- Stir the roasted squash into the tomato mixture, garnish with the coriander and almonds, and serve immediately.

1⟐ Tagine-Spiced Chickpeas with Preserved Lemon Heat 2 tablespoons olive oil in a large frying pan and cook 1 chopped red onion, 2 chopped garlic cloves and 2 teaspoons peeled and finely chopped fresh root ginger for 5–6 minutes, until softened. Stir 2 teaspoons ras el hanout spice blend into the pan with ½ teaspoon sweet paprika and a 400 g (13 oz) can rinsed and drained chickpeas. Stir over a medium heat for 1 minute, then add 3 diced ripe tomatoes, ½ small diced preserved lemon and 2 tablespoons chopped coriander and stir for 2 minutes, until the tomatoes start to collapse. Serve immediately with steamed couscous.

2⟐ Quick Vegetable and Chickpea Tagine Cook the red onion, garlic and ginger as in the 10-minute recipe, then add 2 teaspoons ras el hanout, ½ teaspoon turmeric, 1 teaspoon sweet paprika and a pinch of saffron. Cook for 1 minute, then stir in 2 courgettes, cubed, 250 g (8 oz) cauliflower florets and 50 g (2 oz) chopped apricots, a 400 g (13 oz) can tomatoes, 100 ml (3½ fl oz) hot vegetable stock and a 400 g (13 oz) can rinsed, drained chickpeas. Season and bring to the boil. Cover and simmer for 10–12 minutes.

10 Mussel and Leek Carbonara

Serves 4

2 tablespoons olive oil

200 g (7 oz) streaky bacon
rashers, chopped

1 garlic clove, chopped

2 leeks, split lengthways and
thinly sliced

300 g (10 oz) cooked shelled
mussels

700 g (1 lb 7 oz) fresh spaghetti

2 eggs

150 ml (¼ pint) single cream

black pepper

- Place the oil in a large frying pan and cook the bacon over a medium-high heat for 2–3 minutes, until golden. Reduce the heat slightly, add the garlic and leeks and cook for 4–5 minutes, stirring occasionally, until softened and golden. Add the mussels for the final 1–2 minutes, and stir until hot.

- Meanwhile, cook the spaghetti in a large pan of salted boiling water for 3–4 minutes, or according to the packet instructions, until tender.

- Put the eggs and cream into a bowl with plenty of black pepper and beat together.

- Drain the pasta and toss quickly with the mussel mixture and creamy eggs until well coated. Heap into bowls and serve immediately.

---

2 Mussel, Leek and Potato Gratin

Cook 500 g (1 lb) thinly sliced potatoes in a pan of lightly salted boiling water for 8–10 minutes, until tender. Meanwhile, prepare the mussel and leek sauce as in the main recipe but omit the eggs. Drain the potatoes and combine gently with the prepared sauce and 75 g (3 oz) grated Cheddar or Emmental cheese. Tip into an ovenproof dish, top with a further 75 g (3 oz) grated cheese and slide under a preheated medium-hot grill for 4–5 minutes, until bubbling and golden. Serve with plenty of green salad.

3 Fennel, Leek and Mussel Risotto

Heat 2 tablespoons olive oil in a large pan over a medium-high heat. Cook 150 g (5 oz) chopped bacon for 2–3 minutes, until lightly golden. Reduce the heat slightly, add 1 small, finely chopped fennel bulb and 2 finely sliced leeks and cook for 4–5 minutes, to soften. Stir 350 g (11½ oz) risotto rice into the pan for 1 minute, until the grains are coated and become slightly translucent. Pour in 125 ml (4 fl oz) dry white wine and simmer rapidly, stirring constantly until the wine has evaporated. Add 1.2 litres (2 pints)

boiling fish or vegetable stock a small ladleful at a time, stirring constantly at a gentle simmer until each ladleful has been absorbed. When the rice is 'al dente' (after about 17 minutes), stir in 300 g (10 oz) cooked shelled mussels plus 3 tablespoons crème fraîche. Take off the heat, cover and set aside to rest for 1–2 minutes before serving.

Quick Lamb and Spinach Tikka

Serves 4

2 tablespoons vegetable oil

400 g (13 oz) lean lamb steak or fillet, cut into strips

1 onion, thickly sliced

2 garlic cloves, sliced

2 teaspoons peeled and finely grated fresh root ginger

1 teaspoon cumin seeds

1 large green chilli, finely sliced (deseeded if less heat desired)

2 tablespoons tikka curry paste

3 large ripe tomatoes, roughly chopped

125 ml (4 fl oz) hot lamb or vegetable stock

150 g (5 oz) roughly chopped spinach leaves

flatbreads, to serve

chopped coriander, to garnish

- Place half the oil in a large frying pan over a high heat and stir-fry the lamb for 2–3 minutes, until browned. Using a slotted spoon, transfer to a plate and set aside.

- Return the pan to a medium-high heat and cook the onion, garlic, ginger, cumin seeds and chilli in the remaining oil for 3–4 minutes, until lightly coloured. Reduce the heat slightly, then add the tikka paste, stirring for 1 minute.

- Add the tomatoes and stock and simmer for 5–6 minutes, until the sauce has thickened slightly. Stir in the spinach and heat for a further 1–2 minutes, until wilted.

- Return the lamb to the pan, stir until reheated, then serve sprinkled with coriander, with flatbreads.

Curried Lamb Steaks

Rub 2 tablespoons tandoori curry paste over 4 lamb steaks. Place them on a foil-lined grill rack, slide under a preheated medium-hot grill and cook for 6–8 minutes, turning once, until lightly charred and cooked to your liking. Set aside, covered with foil and rest for 1–2 minutes. Serve with steamed brown basmati rice or chapattis, a tomato and onion salad and a tray of Indian-style pickles.

Lamb and Potato Madras

Heat 2 tablespoons vegetable oil in a large pan over a medium-high heat and brown 400 g (13 oz) cubed, lean lamb steak for 2–3 minutes, until browned. Using a slotted spoon, transfer to a plate and set aside. Return the pan to the heat and cook the onion, garlic, ginger, cumin seeds and chilli from the main recipe for 3–4 minutes, until lightly coloured. Add 2 tablespoons Madras curry paste plus 400 g (13 oz) diced potatoes, cook for 1 minute, then add a 400 g (13 oz) can crushed plum tomatoes and 200 ml (7 fl oz) hot lamb stock. Simmer for 15–18 minutes, or until the potatoes are tender. Return the lamb to the pan with 150 g (5 oz) chopped spinach for the final 2–3 minutes, and cook until the leaves have wilted.

10 Quick Spiced Cauliflower Pilau

Serves 4

25 g (1 oz) raisins

400 g (13 oz) small cauliflower florets

2 tablespoons vegetable oil

2 garlic cloves, crushed

2 spring onions, thinly sliced

1½ tablespoons medium-hot curry paste

500 g (1 lb) ready-cooked steamed pilau rice

chopped coriander leaves, to garnish

flatbreads, to serve (optional)

- Put the raisins into a heatproof bowl, pour in 2 tablespoons boiling water and set aside to soak.

- Cook the cauliflower florets in a large pan of boiling water for 4–5 minutes, until just tender.

- Meanwhile, heat the oil in a large pan and fry the garlic and spring onions over a medium heat for 1 minute to soften. Add the curry paste and stir for 1 minute to cook the spices. Add the steamed rice, the raisins and their water, then cover and cook over a medium-low heat for 2–3 minutes.

- Drain the cauliflower and fold it into the rice. Spoon into dishes, garnish with the coriander and serve accompanied by flatbreads, if desired.

---

20 Spiced Cauliflower Cheese

Cook 900 g (1 lb 13 oz) large cauliflower florets in a large pan of boiling salted water for 8–10 minutes, or until just tender. Drain and place in 1 large or 4 individual ovenproof dishes. Meanwhile, melt 50 g (2 oz) butter in a large pan and add 1 large, finely chopped onion, 2 chopped garlic cloves and 1 teaspoon cumin seeds. Cook for 6–7 minutes over a medium heat, stirring occasionally, until softened. Add 1 teaspoon ground coriander, ½ teaspoon turmeric and ¼ teaspoon cayenne pepper and stir for 1 minute. Mix in 300 ml (½ pint) crème fraîche and 200 g (7 oz) grated mild cheese, such as Gouda, and stir until melted. Season to taste, then pour the sauce over the cauliflower, top with a further 75 g (3 oz) grated Gouda and slide under a preheated medium-hot grill for 5–6 minutes, until bubbling and golden.

30 Aromatic Spiced Cauliflower Stew

Heat 2 tablespoons oil in a pan and cook 1 chopped onion, 2 chopped garlic cloves and 1 teaspoon cumin seeds over a medium heat for 6–7 minutes, stirring occasionally, until softened. Add 2 tablespoons medium-hot curry paste and stir for 1 minute. Add 625 g (1¼ lb) cauliflower florets and a 400 g (13 oz) can rinsed and drained chickpeas and stir. Pour in a 400 g (13 oz) can cherry or plum tomatoes plus 200 ml (7 fl oz) water, then season, cover loosely and simmer for 15–18 minutes, until tender. Serve scattered with chopped coriander and a dollop of natural yogurt.

20 Tuna and Bulgar Wheat Bowl

Serves 4

750 ml (1¼ pints) vegetable stock
300 g (10 oz) bulgar wheat
3 tablespoons olive oil
4 tuna steaks
400 g (13 oz) can kidney beans, drained
125 g (4 oz) drained or defrosted sweetcorn
2 spring onions, finely sliced
2 roasted red peppers, drained and diced
small bunch of coriander, chopped
2 tablespoons lemon juice
salt and pepper

- Pour the stock into a pan, bring to the boil and add the bulgar. Cook, uncovered, over a medium heat, for 7 minutes. Cover with a tight-fitting lid and set aside for 6–7 minutes, until the liquid has been absorbed and the grains are tender.

- Meanwhile, heat a ridged griddle pan over a medium-high heat. Rub 1 tablespoon of the oil over the tuna steaks and season with salt and pepper. Cook them in the griddle pan for 2–3 minutes on each side, until nicely charred and cooked to your liking. Set aside and keep warm.

- Gently stir the remaining ingredients into the bulgar, then replace the lid for 3–4 minutes. Spoon the warm mixture into bowls and serve topped with the griddled tuna.

 Quick Tuna Tabbouleh
Tip 500 g (1 lb) ready-cooked quinoa into a large bowl. Add 3 finely chopped spring onions, 1 finely chopped red pepper, 2 tablespoons chopped parsley, 2 tablespoons chopped mint and 125 g (4 oz) halved cherry tomatoes. Drain and flake 2 x 160 g (5½ oz) cans tuna in olive oil and add to the bowl. Now add 2 tablespoons lemon juice, 2 tablespoons olive oil and a generous pinch of salt and pepper. Stir gently to combine and serve immediately with toasted pitta breads.

 Roasted Pumpkin with Tuna and Bulgar Wheat Peel 500 g (1 lb) pumpkin or squash and chop into 1.5 cm (¾ inch) dice. Place in a large roasting tin, add 2 tablespoons olive oil, 2 unpeeled garlic cloves and 1 sliced red onion and toss together. Season generously and roast in a preheated oven, 220°C (425°F), Gas Mark 7, for 18–20 minutes, until tender. Meanwhile, cook the bulgar wheat and griddle the tuna following the main recipe. Toss the cooked bulgar with the pumpkin, heap into dishes and serve topped with the seared tuna steak and wedges of lemon, if desired.

30 Pork, Red Pepper and Three-Bean Goulash

Serves 4

2 tablespoons olive oil

350 g (11½ oz) pork loin or fillet, cut into thick strips

1 onion, sliced

1 red pepper, diced

2 garlic cloves, chopped

1 tablespoon plain flour

1 tablespoon sweet smoked paprika

400 g (13 oz) can three-bean salad, rinsed and drained

400 g (13 oz) can cherry or chopped tomatoes

1 tablespoon tomato purée

200 ml (7 fl oz) hot vegetable stock

salt and pepper

steamed winter greens, to serve

- Heat half the oil in a large pan over a medium-high heat and cook the pork strips for 3–4 minutes, until browned all over. Using a slotted spoon, transfer to a plate and set aside.

- Return the pan to a medium heat with the remaining oil, then add the onion, red pepper and garlic. Cook for 5–6 minutes, until softened and lightly coloured.

- Reduce the heat slightly, add the flour and paprika and stir for 1 minute. Add the beans, tomatoes, tomato purée and stock, then season and simmer for 15–18 minutes, until rich and thick. Return the pork and its juices to the pan for the final 3–4 minutes, until heated through.

- Serve with steamed winter greens.

Red Pepper and Bacon Bagel

Halve 4 bagels and toast the cut sides. Meanwhile, grill 12 smoked, streaky bacon rashers under a preheated medium-hot grill for 4–5 minutes, turning once. Put 1 teaspoon sweet smoked paprika in a bowl and mix in 1 tablespoon chopped chives and 2 tablespoons mayonnaise. Spread over the bottom half of each bagel. Top with a small handful of baby spinach leaves and 1 drained and sliced roasted red pepper. Arrange the bacon over the pepper and top with the remaining bagel halves.

Red Pepper, Pancetta and Bean

Frittata Heat 2 tablespoons olive oil in a large, ovenproof frying pan and cook 150 g (5 oz) cubed pancetta over a medium-high heat for 2–3 minutes, until golden. Add 3 drained and sliced roasted red peppers, a 400 g (13 oz) can rinsed and drained three-bean salad and 50 g (2 oz) drained and chopped sun-dried tomatoes. Stir for 2–3 minutes until hot, then reduce the heat to medium-low. Add 4 large beaten eggs with a pinch of salt and pepper and 1 tablespoon chopped chives and stir to combine. Cook gently, without stirring, for 4–5 minutes, until the egg is almost set, then sprinkle with 150 g (5 oz) mature grated Cheddar cheese. Slide under a preheated medium-hot grill for 3–4 minutes, until puffed up and golden. Serve in wedges on a bed of steamed winter greens.

King Prawn Soba Noodles with Sweet and Sour Dressing

Serves 2

300 g (10 oz) raw peeled
  king prawns
175 g (6 oz) soba noodles
½ cucumber, deseeded and
  finely shredded
1–2 spring onions, thinly shredded
small bunch of coriander leaves
blanched peanuts, to scatter

For the dressing

2 tablespoons lime juice
1 teaspoon fish sauce
1 tablespoon caster sugar
2 tablespoons sweet chilli sauce

- Arrange the prawns in a steamer over a pan of gently simmering water and steam for 3–5 minutes, until pink and cooked. Rinse under cold water to cool and set aside.

- Bring a large pan of water to the boil and cook the noodles for 5–7 minutes, or according to the packet instructions, until tender. Drain and rinse immediately under cold water.

- Meanwhile, combine the dressing ingredients and stir until the sugar has dissolved.

- Toss the noodles in half the dressing, then combine with the cooked prawns, cucumber, spring onions and coriander.

- Heap into dishes and scatter with the peanuts. Serve drizzled with extra dressing, as desired.

 Brown Egg-Fried Rice with Sweet and Sour Prawns Place 1 tablespoon oil in a wok over a medium heat and stir-fry 1 sliced garlic clove, 2 teaspoons peeled and chopped fresh root ginger and 1 sliced red chilli for 2 minutes. Beat 1 egg with 2 teaspoons soy sauce and add to the pan, stirring occasionally, for 1–2 minutes. Add 50 g (2 oz) peas, 50 g (2 oz) sweetcorn and 250 g (8 oz) steamed brown basmati rice. Stir-fry for 3–4 minutes. Meanwhile, warm 195 g (6¾ oz) sweet and sour sauce in a pan with 200 g (13 oz) cooked peeled prawns for 2–3 minutes. Divide the rice between 2 dishes and spoon over the prawns.

King Prawn and Brown Rice Stir-Fry with Sweet and Sour Sauce Cook 100 g (3½ oz) rinsed brown rice in a large pan of salted boiling water for 20–25 minutes, or according to the packet instructions, until tender. Add 50 g (2 oz) defrosted peas and 50 g (2 oz) defrosted sweetcorn for the final 2 minutes, then drain well. Meanwhile, lightly beat 1 large egg with 2 teaspoons soy sauce. Heat 2 tablespoons oil in a large wok and stir-fry 1 sliced garlic clove, 2 teaspoons peeled and chopped fresh root ginger and 1 deseeded and sliced red chilli (optional) for 1–2 minutes over a medium heat, until lightly coloured. Add 200 g (8 oz) peeled king prawns and stir-fry for 2–3 minutes, until pink. Pour the egg into the pan and stir-fry for 1–2 minutes, until set. Tip the rice and vegetables into the wok, stir-fry for a further 2–3 minutes, until hot, then spoon into dishes. Serve immediately, drizzled with about 195 g (6¾ oz) warmed sweet and sour or sweet chilli sauce.

30 Red Cabbage and Beetroot Tagine

Serves 4–6

2 tablespoons olive oil

1 red onion, sliced

2 garlic cloves, finely chopped

1 small red cabbage, shredded

500 g (1 lb) raw beetroot, peeled and cut into 1 cm (½ inch) dice

1 small cinnamon stick

generous pinch of saffron

1 teaspoon cumin seeds

400 ml (14 fl oz) hot lamb, chicken or vegetable stock

50 g (2 oz) green olives

½ small preserved lemon, chopped

salt and pepper

chopped coriander or parsley, to garnish

steamed wholewheat couscous or bulgar wheat, to serve

- Heat the oil in a large, flameproof casserole dish and cook the onion and garlic over a medium heat for 6–7 minutes, until softened slightly. Add the red cabbage, beetroot, spices and seasoning and stir for a further 1–2 minutes, until aromatic.

- Pour in the stock, season lightly, cover and simmer gently over a medium-low heat for 15–20 minutes, until the vegetables are tender. Stir in the olives and lemon for the final 10 minutes.

- Garnish the tagine with the chopped herbs and serve with the couscous or bulgar.

---

10 Tagine-Spiced Red Cabbage and Beetroot Salad

Shred ½ small head red cabbage. Place in a bowl with 300 g (10 oz) raw, peeled and coarsely grated beetroot and 1 peeled and coarsely grated dessert apple. In a separate bowl, combine 2 teaspoons lemon juice with 3 tablespoons olive oil, 1 teaspoon toasted cumin seeds, a pinch of ground cinnamon and a pinch of salt and pepper. Toss the dressing with the salad ingredients and serve scattered with 2 tablespoons chopped parsley or coriander.

20 Spiced Braised Red Cabbage and Beetroot

Heat 2 tablespoons oil in a large pan and cook 1 finely sliced red onion and 2 chopped garlic cloves for 5–6 minutes, until softened. Add 1 teaspoon cumin seeds, 1 teaspoon sweet paprika and ½ teaspoon ground ginger and cook for 1 minute. Stir in 1 small head finely shredded red cabbage, 400 g (13 oz) peeled and coarsely grated raw beetroot, 1 peeled and coarsely grated dessert apple and 50 g (2 oz) chopped, stoned dates (optional). Stir until hot, then pour in 400 ml (14 fl oz) hot chicken or vegetable stock with 2 teaspoons lemon juice. Simmer for 10–12 minutes, stirring occasionally, until the vegetables have softened slightly. Season to taste and serve as a side dish or accompanied by steamed couscous or bulgar wheat.

20 Stir-Fried Lemon Chicken with Toasted Cashews

Serves 2

1 tablespoon groundnut oil
250 (8 oz) skinless chicken
  breasts, sliced
125 g (4 oz) broccoli florets
1 small red pepper, roughly
  chopped
2 spring onions, thickly sliced
50 g (2 oz) unsalted cashew nuts
1 tablespoon cornflour
125 ml (4 fl oz) cold water
2 tablespoons lemon juice
1½ tablespoons honey
2 tablespoons light soy sauce
steamed rice or noodles, to serve
  (optional)

- Heat the oil in a large wok or frying pan and cook the chicken for 3–4 minutes over a medium-high heat, until golden. Using a slotted spoon, transfer to a plate and set aside.

- Return the pan to the heat and add the broccoli, red pepper and spring onions. Stir-fry for 3–4 minutes, until softened.

- Meanwhile, place a small pan over a medium-low heat and toast the cashew nuts for 3–4 minutes, shaking the pan occasionally, until golden. Remove from the heat.

- Dissolve the cornflour in a small bowl with 1 tablespoon of the water, then mix in the remaining water plus the lemon juice, honey and soy sauce. Add to the vegetables along with the cashew nuts. Reduce the heat to medium-low and return the chicken to the pan. Simmer for 2–3 minutes, until the chicken is cooked through and the sauce hot and thickened. Serve immediately, with steamed rice or noodles, if desired.

---

10 Crunchy Lemon Chicken Salad

Place 2 teaspoons grated lemon rind in a dish with 75 g (3 oz) breadcrumbs. Place 50 g (2 oz) plain flour in a second dish and 1 beaten egg in a third. Dip 250 g (8 oz) chicken mini fillets first in the flour, then the egg and finally the breadcrumbs, until coated. Heat 2 tablespoons oil in a frying pan and cook the mini fillets for 7–8 minutes, turning occasionally, until golden. Serve with mixed salad leaves, sprinkled with 2 tablespoons toasted cashew nuts and 1 thinly sliced spring onion, and desired dressing.

30 Lemony Baked Stir-Fry Chicken

Season 2 diced chicken breasts with salt and pepper, then place in a bowl with 2 teaspoons groundnut oil and 1 teaspoon sesame oil. Add 1 roughly chopped small red pepper, ½ sliced onion and 1.5 cm (¾ inch) piece of peeled fresh root ginger cut into matchsticks. Toss everything together, then tip into a large roasting tin and bake in a preheated oven, 200°C (400°F), Gas Mark 6, for 10 minutes, turning occasionally. Toss 125 g (4 oz) broccoli florets into the tin and cook for a further 5 minutes. Meanwhile, combine the sauce ingredients from the main recipe and pour into the roasting tin with the toasted cashews from the main recipe for a final 5 minutes, until the chicken is cooked and the sauce is sticky. Serve with rice or noodles.

3️ Salmon and Lentil Fishcakes

Serves 4

2 x 170 g (5¾ oz) cans salmon, drained

400 g (13 oz) can green lentils in water, drained

2 tablespoons chopped herbs, such as parsley or chives

2 eggs

50 g (2 oz) fine breadcrumbs

2 tablespoons olive oil

salt and pepper

To serve

green salad

aïoli or tartare sauce (optional)

lemon wedges

- Place the salmon, lentils, herbs and eggs in a food processor or bowl, add some seasoning, then pulse or stir to combine. Form into 8 fishcakes and coat in the breadcrumbs. Arrange on a plate and chill for 12–15 minutes to firm up.

- Heat the oil in a large frying pan over a medium heat and fry the fishcakes for about 4–5 minutes, turning once, until crisp and golden. Drain on kitchen paper and serve with green salad and aïoli or tartare sauce, if desired, and lemon wedges for squeezing over.

 Warm Salmon and Puy Lentil Salad Heat 2 tablespoons olive oil in a frying pan and cook 2 chopped garlic cloves and 3 sliced spring onions for 2–3 minutes, until softened. Add 50 g (2 oz) chopped sun-dried tomatoes to the pan with 2 tablespoons chopped parsley and 500 g (1 lb) ready-cooked Puy lentils. Stir over the heat for 3–4 minutes, then add 185 g (6½ oz) flaked roast salmon fillets and 1 tablespoon lemon juice. Stir gently to warm through, then spoon into 4 dishes and top each serving with a small handful of rocket leaves and 2 slices of feta, if desired.

 Herby Crust Salmon with Lentils Place 50 g (2 oz) freshly made breadcrumbs in a bowl with 2 tablespoons chopped parsley, 1 teaspoon grated lemon rind, 1 tablespoon finely chopped sun-dried tomatoes and 2 finely chopped spring onions. Add 1 tablespoon olive oil and mix well to combine. Place 4 boneless salmon fillets in a shallow ovenproof dish and cover with the herby topping. Place in a preheated oven, 200°C (400°F), Gas Mark 6, for 12–15 minutes, until cooked and golden. Serve immediately with 500 g (1 lb) warmed ready-cooked Puy lentils and a rocket and feta salad.

 # Cold-Busting Chilli Beef Burgers

Serves 4

400 g (13 oz) minced beef
½ small red onion, finely chopped
1 green chilli, deseeded and chopped
2 tablespoons mixed chopped herbs
1 egg, lightly beaten
2 teaspoons Mexican spice blend
1 teaspoon Tabasco sauce
50 g (2 oz) fresh breadcrumbs
salt and pepper
2 tablespoons sunflower oil

To serve

wholegrain burger buns
selection of toppings, such as
   salsa, avocado and lettuce

- Combine all the burger ingredients in a large bowl and mix well. Form into 4 large patties about 1.5 cm (¾ inch) thick.

- Heat the oil in a large frying pan and cook the burgers over a medium heat for 8–12 minutes, turning once, until cooked to your liking.

- Serve in the burger buns with a choice of toppings, as left.

 Cold-Busting Chilli Beef Tostadas
Rub 2 teaspoons olive oil and 2 teaspoons Mexican-style spice blend over 2 sirloin steaks. Heat 1 tablespoon oil in a frying pan and cook the steaks over a medium-high heat for 4–7 minutes. Set aside. Meanwhile, toast 4 tortillas under a preheated medium-hot grill for 2–3 minutes. Place on plates and spread 2 tablespoons salsa over each. Sprinkle with 100 g (3½ oz) grated Cheddar, ½ sliced red onion, ½ head shredded iceberg and 1 diced avocado. Slice the beef, arrange over the lettuce and serve topped with chopped coriander, Tabasco sauce and a squeeze of lime juice.

 Cold-Busting Chocolate Chilli Beef Heat 2 tablespoons vegetable oil in a large pan and cook 1 chopped onion, 1 chopped red pepper and 2 chopped garlic cloves over a medium-high heat for 4–5 minutes, until slightly softened. Add 400 g (13 oz) minced beef and cook for 3–4 minutes, until browned. Stir in a 41 g (1½ oz) packet chilli con carne spice mix, a 400 g (13 oz) can chopped tomatoes, a 400 g (13 oz) can drained kidney beans, 100 ml (3½ fl oz) red wine and 100 ml (3½ fl oz) water. Bring to the boil, then reduce the heat and stir in 2 squares (about 15 g/½ oz total weight) dark chocolate (minimum 85% cocoa solids), until melted. Cover loosely and simmer for 15–18 minutes, until rich and thick. Scatter over 2 tablespoons chopped coriander and serve with warmed tortillas, Tabasco sauce and lime wedges.

Spiced Cabbage and Bacon Pan-Fry

Serves 2

2 tablespoons olive oil
100 g (3½ oz) thick bacon rashers,
  cut into 1 cm (½ inch) strips
1 small onion, finely sliced
2 garlic cloves, chopped
pinch of ground allspice
pinch of ground cinnamon
¼ teaspoon grated nutmeg
½ small head Savoy cabbage,
  thinly shredded
200 g (7 oz) cauliflower florets
salt and pepper
2 tablespoons chopped parsley,
  to garnish

- Heat the oil in a large frying pan and cook the bacon for 2–3 minutes over a medium-high heat, until golden. Add the onion and garlic and cook for a further 3–4 minutes, until beginning to soften.

- Stir in the spices until aromatic, then add the cabbage and cauliflower and stir-fry for 7–8 minutes, until slightly softened but still with some bite. Season to taste, garnish with parsley, then heap into deep bowls to serve.

 Spiced Cabbage Coleslaw with Crispy Bacon Core ½ small head white cabbage and slice thinly. Place in a large bowl with 1 grated carrot, 1 finely sliced celery stick, 150 g (5 oz) finely sliced cauliflower florets and 2 thinly sliced spring onions. In a separate small bowl, combine 150 ml (¼ pint) soured cream, 2 teaspoons lemon juice, a pinch of ground allspice, cinnamon and nutmeg, 2 tablespoons chopped parsley and salt and pepper to taste. Pour the dressing over the vegetables and mix well. Crumble over 50 g (2 oz) cooked smoked bacon strips and serve with toasted pitta breads or baked potatoes, if desired.

 Spiced Red Cabbage with Gammon Melt 50 g (2 oz) butter in a large pan and gently cook 1 sliced onion and 1 chopped garlic clove over a medium-low heat for 5–6 minutes, until softened. Stir in the spices from the main recipe with ½ small head shredded red cabbage and 1 peeled, cored and grated dessert apple. Cook gently for about 15 minutes, stirring frequently, until slightly softened. Meanwhile, rub 4 gammon steaks with a little oil and arrange on a foil-lined grill rack. Slide under a preheated medium-hot grill for 12–15 minutes, turning once, until cooked and golden but still juicy. Keep warm and set aside to rest for 2–3 minutes before serving with the spiced red cabbage.

30 Chestnut Mushroom and Spinach Pilau

Serves 4

2 tablespoons vegetable oil

1 onion, finely chopped

2 garlic cloves, finely chopped

200 g (7 oz) chestnut
  mushrooms, diced

3 cardamom pods, lightly crushed

¼ teaspoon ground cloves

½ teaspoon ground cinnamon

150 g (5 oz) basmati rice

500 ml (17 fl oz) hot vegetable
  stock

125 g (4 oz) frozen peas,
  defrosted

125 g (4 oz) spinach leaves,
  roughly chopped

salt and pepper

fried onions, to garnish (optional)

- Heat the oil in a large, deep-sided frying pan and cook the onion and garlic for 4–5 minutes over a medium-high heat, stirring occasionally, until beginning to colour.

- Add the mushrooms, cook for 2 minutes, then add the spices and rice and stir for 1 minute.

- Pour in the stock, season generously and cover with a tight-fitting lid. Simmer very gently for about 15 minutes, until the rice grains are almost tender.

- Remove from the heat and fold in the peas and spinach. Replace the lid and set aside for 4–5 minutes, until the liquid has been absorbed and the rice is tender and light.

- Serve garnished with fried onions, if desired.

---

10 Mushrooms and Spinach with Brown

Rice Heat 2 tablespoons vegetable oil in a large frying pan and cook the onion, garlic and mushrooms following the main recipe. Meanwhile, heat 500 g (1 lb) steamed brown basmati rice according to the packet instructions. Stir the spices from the main recipe into the onions, then add 125 g (4 oz) roughly chopped spinach and stir-fry for 1–2 minutes, until wilted. Fold through the rice and serve with a dollop of Greek yogurt, and garnished with fried onions, if desired.

20 Warm Mushroom and Spinach Pâté

Melt 75 g (3 oz) butter in a large frying pan and cook 2 chopped garlic cloves and 500 g (1 lb) diced chestnut mushrooms over a medium-low heat for 5–6 minutes, until tender. Stir in 150 g (5 oz) chopped spinach and set aside to cool for 10 minutes. Place 150 g (5 oz) cream cheese in a food processor with a pinch of ground cloves and ground cinnamon and 2 tablespoons chopped parsley. Season with salt and pepper, then add the mushrooms and spinach and pulse briefly to create a slightly warm, chunky-textured pâté. If you don't have a processor, put the cooked mushroom and spinach mixture into a bowl, beat in the cream cheese, spices and parsley and season with salt and pepper. Spoon into ramekins and serve with warmed naan breads or chapattis.

20 Quick Fish Stew with Chickpeas

Serves 4

2 tablespoons olive oil
1 celery stick, thinly sliced
2 garlic cloves, chopped
1 teaspoon sweet paprika
125 ml (4 fl oz) dry white wine
400 g (13 oz) can good-quality
   ratatouille
400 g (13 oz) chickpeas
1 teaspoon grated lemon rind
75 ml (3 fl oz) vegetable stock
400 g (13 oz) boneless fish fillets,
   such as haddock, cod or salmon,
   cut into bite-sized pieces
salt and pepper
chopped parsley, to garnish
steamed wholegrain rice or
   couscous, to serve

- Heat the oil in a large saucepan and cook the celery and garlic over a medium heat for 3–4 minutes, to soften.

- Add the paprika, stir for 1 minute, then pour in the wine and simmer to reduce by half.

- Tip in the ratatouille along with the chickpeas, lemon rind and stock, then season to taste and simmer for 5–6 minutes, to thicken slightly.

- Stir the fish into the stew, cover and simmer for a further 3–5 minutes, or until the fish is cooked and flaky. Garnish with chopped parsley and serve with rice or couscous.

 Pan-Fried Fish with Chickpea Ratatouille Heat 2 tablespoons oil in a large frying pan and fry 4 boneless, skinless fish fillets, such as cod, haddock or salmon, for 5–7 minutes, turning once, until the fish is cooked and flaky. Meanwhile, in a separate pan, heat a 400 g (13 oz) can ratatouille with a 400 g (13 oz) can rinsed and drained chickpeas, 1 teaspoon finely grated lemon rind and 100 ml (3½ fl oz) hot vegetable stock. Season to taste and simmer for 4–5 minutes, to allow the flavours to develop. Spoon into shallow dishes and serve immediately, topped with the fish and garnished with parsley.

 One-Pot Baked Fish with Chickpeas Prepare the stew following the main recipe, adding 1 small diced head of fennel to the celery and garlic and cooking for 5–6 minutes before adding the paprika. Once the stew has simmered for 5–6 minutes, transfer it to an ovenproof dish and place 4 skinless, boneless fish fillets on top. Drizzle with 1 tablespoon olive oil, season and bake, uncovered, in a preheated oven, 200°C (400°F), Gas Mark 6, for 12–15 minutes. Serve with rice or couscous and garnished with chopped parsley.

20 Sausages with Sprout Colcannon

Serves 2

4 flavoured sausages, such as
  pork and apple
400 g (13 oz) floury potatoes,
  cut into chunks
50 g (2 oz) butter
200 g (7 oz) Brussels sprouts,
  sliced or shredded
¼ teaspoon freshly grated
  nutmeg
1 tablespoon chopped chives
1 tablespoon wholegrain mustard
2 tablespoons crème fraîche
salt and pepper

- Arrange the sausages on a foil-lined grill rack and slide under a preheated, medium-hot grill for 15–18 minutes, or according to the packet instructions, until cooked through.

- Cook the potatoes in a pan of salted boiling water for 12–15 minutes, until tender.

- Meanwhile, melt half the butter in a frying pan and cook the sprouts with the nutmeg and a generous pinch of salt and pepper over a medium-low heat for 4–6 minutes, stirring occasionally, until softened.

- Drain the potatoes, return to the pan and mash until smooth with the remaining butter. Stir in the chives, mustard, crème fraîche and sprouts and serve with the grilled sausages.

---

10 Quick Sausage and Sprout Pan-Fry

Blanch 250 g (8 oz) halved Brussels sprouts in a large pan of salted boiling water for 2–3 minutes, until just beginning to soften, then drain well. Meanwhile, heat 2 tablespoons olive oil in a large frying pan and cook 2 chopped garlic cloves over a medium-low heat for 1–2 minutes, until softened. Add 225 g (7½ oz) cooked sliced sausages and the drained sprouts, then stir-fry over a medium-high heat for a further 3–4 minutes, until just tender and golden. Serve with warmed colcannon or mashed potato.

30 One-Pan Sausage Roast with Sprouts

Arrange 350 g (11½ oz) thickly sliced herby sausages in a large roasting tin with 250 g (8 oz) Brussels sprouts, 2 unpeeled garlic cloves, 1 small red onion cut into wedges and 2 thyme sprigs. Season, drizzle over 2 tablespoons olive oil and mix to coat. Roast in a preheated oven, 220°C (425°F), Gas Mark 7, for 20–25 minutes, turning occasionally, until cooked and golden. Meanwhile, prepare the mustardy mashed potatoes from the main recipe, omitting the sprouts. Serve the one-pan roast with the mashed potatoes.

20 Spicy Sardine Linguine

Serves 4

2 tablespoons olive oil

1 red onion, chopped

2 garlic cloves, crushed

400 g (13 oz) can cherry
  tomatoes

½ teaspoon dried chilli flakes

pinch of sugar

½ teaspoon finely grated
  lemon rind

350 g (11½ oz) linguine

2 x 120 g (3¾ oz) cans sardines
  in oil, drained

2 teaspoons rinsed capers

salt and pepper

basil leaves, to garnish
  (optional)

- Heat the olive oil in a large pan and cook the onion and garlic over a medium heat for 6–7 minutes, until softened. Add the tomatoes, chilli flakes, sugar, lemon rind and seasoning and bring to the boil. Cover and simmer for about 10 minutes, until thickened.

- Meanwhile, cook the linguine in a large pan of boiling salted water for 11 minutes, or according to the packet instructions, until 'al dente'. Drain, reserving 2 tablespoons of the cooking water and return to the pan.

- Stir the sardines and capers into the tomato sauce for the final 1–2 minutes. When hot, add to the drained pasta along with the reserved cooking water and toss gently. Serve heaped into bowls and garnished with extra black pepper, and with basil leaves, if desired.

 Quick Spicy Sardine Spaghetti

Cook 700 g (1 lb 7 oz) fresh spaghetti in a large pan of boiling salted water for 3–4 minutes, or according to the packet instructions, until 'al dente'. Drain, reserving 3 tablespoons of the cooking water. Meanwhile, heat 2 tablespoons olive oil in a pan and fry 2 chopped garlic cloves and 1 chopped red chilli (deseeded if less heat desired) over a medium-low heat for 1–2 minutes, until softened but not coloured. Add 2 x 120 g (3¾ oz) cans drained, flaked sardines in oil, 1 tablespoon lemon juice and 2 teaspoons rinsed capers. Warm through for 2–3 minutes, then pour over the spaghetti, add the reserved cooking water and 2 tablespoons chopped parsley or basil and toss together. Season to taste and serve.

Spicy Tomato and Sardine Pasta Bake

Make the tomato sauce with sardines following the main recipe, but reducing the simmering time to 5 minutes so that the sauce is less thick. Meanwhile, cook 300 g (10 oz) penne pasta in a large pan of boiling salted water until 'al dente'. Stir into the sauce, tip into a large, ovenproof dish and top with 125 g (4 oz) halved mini mozzarella balls. Bake in a preheated oven, 200°C (400°F), Gas Mark 6, for 15–18 minutes, or until golden and bubbling.

QuickCook

Comfort-Food Main Meals

Recipes listed by cooking time

3⓪

2⓪

10

 Creamy Butternut and Sage Risini

Serves 4

50 g (2 oz) butter
2–3 banana shallots, chopped
2 garlic cloves, chopped
300 g (10 oz) peeled butternut
  squash, finely chopped
250 g risini or orzo pasta
3 tablespoons pine nuts
700 ml (1 pint 3½ fl oz) hot
  vegetable stock
½ tablespoon chopped sage
125 g (4 oz) mascarpone
25 g (1 oz) freshly grated
  Parmesan cheese
salt and pepper

To garnish

shredded sage leaves
Parmesan shavings (optional)

- Melt the butter in a large, deep-sided frying pan and cook the shallots, garlic and squash over a medium heat for 6–7 minutes. Stir in the risini or orzo until coated.

- Meanwhile, toast the pine nuts in a small, dry frying pan over a medium-low heat for 3–4 minutes, shaking the pan frequently, until golden. Tip on to a small plate and set aside.

- Pour the stock into the risini, add the sage and a generous pinch of salt and pepper. Bring to the boil, then cover with a lid and simmer for about 10 minutes, stirring occasionally to prevent sticking, until the liquid has been absorbed and the squash and pasta are tender.

- Stir the mascarpone and grated Parmesan into the risini and set aside to rest for 1–2 minutes.

- Spoon the mixture into bowls and scatter with the toasted pine nuts, the shredded sage leaves and a few Parmesan shavings, if desired.

10 Cheat's Sage Risotto with Pine Nuts

Melt 50 g (2 oz) butter in a frying pan and cook 3 chopped shallots and 2 chopped garlic cloves for 3–4 minutes, until softened. Toast the pine nuts as in the main recipe. Stir 500 g (1 lb) ready-cooked wholegrain rice into the pan with 75 ml (3 fl oz) hot vegetable stock, 125 g (4 oz) mascarpone, 1 tablespoon chopped sage and 3 tablespoons grated Parmesan cheese. Season to taste and simmer for 2–3 minutes, until hot and creamy. Serve as above.

30 Rainy-Day Butternut and Sage Risotto

Melt 50 g (2 oz) butter in a large frying pan and cook 3 finely chopped banana shallots, 2 chopped garlic cloves and 300 g (10 oz) peeled and finely diced butternut squash for 6–7 minutes, until softened. Add 1 tablespoon chopped sage with 350 g (11½ oz) risotto rice and stir until the grains are coated and looking translucent. Pour in 125 ml (4 fl oz) dry white wine and simmer rapidly, stirring until completely evaporated. Add 1.2 litres (2 pints) boiling vegetable stock a ladleful at a time, stirring constantly at a gentle simmer until each ladleful has been absorbed and the rice is 'al dente'. This process should take about 17 minutes. Stir 2 tablespoons mascarpone into the risotto, then cover and set aside to rest for 1–2 minutes before serving as above.

10 Pan-Fried Polenta Chips with Arrabbiata Sauce

Serves 2

500 g (1 lb) shop-bought polenta

3 tablespoons plain flour, for dusting

4 tablespoons olive oil

375 g (12 oz) carton shop-bought arrabbiata pasta sauce

rocket and Parmesan salad, to serve

- Cut the block of polenta into chip-shaped fingers and dust in the flour, shaking off the excess.

- Heat the oil in a frying pan and cook the polenta chips over a medium-high heat for 2–3 minutes on each side, until crisp and golden. Drain on kitchen paper and keep warm.

- Meanwhile, heat the arrabbiata sauce in a pan. Spoon into small bowls and serve with the polenta chips and salad.

2 Soft Polenta Arrabbiata

Heat 2 tablespoons olive oil in a large pan over a medium heat and cook 1 small chopped red onion, 1 chopped garlic clove and 1 chopped red chilli for 6–7 minutes, until softened. Add 2 ripe diced tomatoes, 50 g (2 oz) sliced pitted green olives and 2 tablespoons chopped parsley. Season with salt and pepper and stir occasionally for 3–4 minutes, until the tomatoes begin to collapse. Meanwhile, cook 125 g (4 oz) quick-cook polenta according to the packet instructions, until soft. Stir in 2 tablespoons grated Parmesan cheese, 1 tablespoon chopped parsley and a generous pinch of salt and pepper, then spoon the polenta into dishes. Serve with the warm arrabbiata sauce, a rocket salad and extra Parmesan, if desired.

3 Arrabbiata Polenta Bake

Pour half a 375 g (12 oz) carton arrabbiata sauce into the bottom of a medium ovenproof dish. Lay 300 g (10 oz) sliced polenta over the sauce and top with 50 g (2 oz) diced mozzarella and 2 tablespoons grated Parmesan. Pour over the remaining sauce and top with 75 g (3 oz) diced mozzarella and 2 tablespoons grated Parmesan. Bake in a preheated oven, 220°C (425°F), Gas Mark 7, for 20–25 minutes, until golden and bubbling. Serve with a salad, as above.

30 Rich and Comforting Baked Beans with Sausages

Serves 4

2 tablespoons olive oil
200 g (7 oz) chopped pancetta
 or bacon
2 banana shallots, finely chopped
2 garlic cloves, chopped
1 celery stick, thinly sliced
1 carrot, diced
1 teaspoon sweet paprika
125 ml (4 fl oz) red wine
2 x 400 g (13 oz) cans haricot
 or cannellini beans, rinsed
 and drained
500 g (1 lb) passata
1 teaspoon red wine vinegar
1 tablespoon Worcestershire sauce
1 tablespoon dark brown sugar
salt and pepper
8 herby sausages, grilled, to serve

- Heat the oil in a large pan and cook the pancetta over a medium-high heat for 3–4 minutes, until golden. Add the shallots, garlic, celery and carrot. Cook for 7–8 minutes, until softened, adding the paprika for the final minute.

- Pour in the wine and simmer until completely evaporated, Add the beans, passata, vinegar, Worcestershire sauce and sugar. Season to taste and simmer for about 15 minutes, stirring occasionally, until rich and thick, adding a little water if necessary.

- Slice the sausages thickly and serve with the beans.

 Smoky Sausage and Beans on Garlic Toast Heat 2 tablespoons olive oil in a large frying pan and cook 1 finely chopped onion and 1 thinly sliced celery stick for 6–7 minutes, to soften. Add 225 g (7½ oz) thickly sliced smoked pork sausage and 1 teaspoon sweet smoked paprika and cook for 1 minute. Add a 400 g (13 oz) can haricot beans plus 500 g (1 lb) shop-bought tomato and basil pasta sauce. Bring to the boil and serve spooned over toasted garlic bread slices.

 Quick Baked Eggs and Beans Prepare the beans following the 10-minute recipe, but omitting the sausage. Divide the mixture between 4 individual ovenproof dishes, then crack an egg into the centre of each one. Bake in a preheated oven, 200°C (400°F), Gas Mark 6, for 8–10 minutes, until the egg white is set but the yolk still soft. Serve with grilled sausages and crusty garlic bread, if desired.

WIN-COMF-WOU

 # Chicken and Brie Puff Pie

Serves 4

320 g (10¾ oz) ready-rolled sheet of puff pastry
1 small egg, beaten
1 tablespoon olive oil
2 leeks, chopped
150 g (5 oz) baby button mushrooms, halved
350 g (11½ oz) cooked chicken, diced
100 g (3½ oz) Brie cheese, sliced
4 slices of prosciutto, cut into strips
1 teaspoon chopped thyme leaves (optional)
4 tablespoons half-fat crème fraîche
salt and pepper

- Line a baking sheet with baking paper. Unroll the pastry, place a pie dish on it upside down and cut around it. Place the pastry on the prepared sheet, brush with beaten egg and bake in a preheated oven, 200°C (400°F), Gas Mark 6, for about 10 minutes, until puffed up and pale golden.

- Meanwhile, heat the oil in a large frying pan and cook the leeks for 3–4 minutes, until softened. Add the mushrooms and cook for a further 3–4 minutes, until soft and golden. Add the remaining ingredients and season to taste.

- Once the chicken is hot, put the filling into the pie dish, top with the pastry lid and return to the oven for 3–4 minutes, or until the pastry is golden and crisp.

 ### Chicken, Brie and Thyme

Melts Split 1 baguette in half lengthways and then widthways to make 4 equal pieces. Spread each cut side with 2 tablespoons onion chutney. Take 200 g (7 oz) chunky sliced chicken, 150 g (5 oz) sliced Brie, 150 g (5 oz) halved cherry tomatoes and 1 teaspoon thyme leaves and place equal amounts of each on the bread. Drizzle each slice with ½ teaspoon olive oil, place on a rack and slide under a preheated medium-hot grill for 5–6 minutes, until melted and golden. Serve with rocket leaves.

 ### Chicken, Brie and Leek Pies

Melt 50 g (2 oz) butter in a large frying pan over a medium heat and cook 2 sliced leeks and 150 g (5 oz) sliced mushrooms for 6–7 minutes, until softened. Meanwhile, unroll a 375 g (12 oz) sheet of shop-bought puff pastry and cut into 4 circles a little larger than the top of 4 individual pie dishes. Cut 4 roasted chicken breasts into bite-sized pieces and add to the pan with 4 slices prosciutto cut into strips, 1 teaspoon chopped thyme and 150 ml (¼ pint) single cream. Heat to boiling point, then divide between the pie dishes. Slice 125 g (4 oz) Brie and put 1 or 2 slices on top of the filling. Cover each dish with a pastry lid, allowing it to overhang slightly. Brush with beaten egg, cut a steam-hole in the top and bake in a preheated oven, 200°C (400°F), Gas Mark 6, for about 15 minutes, until the pastry is puffed up and golden.

20 Crispy Pork Milanese with Root Vegetable Coleslaw

Serves 4

8 pork fillet medallions
3 tablespoons plain flour, seasoned
2 small eggs, beaten
100 g (3½ oz) fresh breadcrumbs
200 g (7 oz) parsnips, coarsely grated
400 g (13 oz) carrots, coarsely grated
1 small dessert apple, peeled, cored and coarsely grated
1 tablespoon chopped dill or parsley
4 tablespoons crème fraîche
1 tablespoon wholegrain mustard
2 teaspoons cider vinegar
3 tablespoons olive oil
salt and pepper
lemon wedges, to garnish

- Place the pork medallions between 2 large pieces of clingfilm and bash with a rolling pin to flatten them to a thickness of 5 mm (¼ inch).

- Place the flour, eggs and breadcrumbs in three separate shallow dishes. Dip the pork first in the flour, then the egg and finally the breadcrumbs.

- Put the parsnips, carrots and apple into a bowl, add the dill, crème fraîche, mustard, vinegar and a pinch of salt and pepper and mix well.

- Heat the oil in a large frying pan and cook the medallions over a medium heat for 4–5 minutes, turning once, until cooked and golden. Spoon the coleslaw on to plates and serve with the crispy pork Milanese, garnished with lemon wedges.

10 **Pan-Fried Pork with Root Vegetable Coleslaw** Heat 2 tablespoons olive oil in a frying pan and cook 4 seasoned pork loin steaks for 3–4 minutes each side, or until cooked and golden. Meanwhile, prepare the coleslaw following the main recipe. Serve with the pan-fried pork.

30 **Roasted Pork Fillet with Root Vegetable Mash** Cut 2 thin pork tenderloins in half. Slice 2 garlic cloves into little matchsticks. Make small slits in the pork and stuff with the garlic and the leaves from 1 rosemary sprig. Place in a small roasting tin and drizzle with 1 tablespoon olive oil. Season with salt and pepper and place in a preheated oven, 220°C (425°F), Gas Mark 7, for 15–20 minutes, until just cooked. Meanwhile, chop 1 kg (2 lb) root vegetables, such as potatoes, parsnips, celeriac and carrots, into chunks and cook in a large pan of lightly salted water for 12–15 minutes, until tender. Drain and return to the pan with 2 tablespoons crème fraîche, 1 tablespoon wholegrain mustard, 2 tablespoons chopped parsley and a generous pinch of salt and pepper. Mash until smooth and keep warm. Remove the pork from the oven and set aside to rest for 1–2 minutes, before serving with the root vegetable mash.

3 Cheesy Tuna and Chive Pasties

Serves 4

50 g (2 oz) butter
2 leeks, finely sliced
500 g (1 lb) shop-bought
  puff pastry
flour, for dusting
2 x 185 g (6½ oz) cans tuna
  in olive oil, drained
175 g (6 oz) cold mashed potato
100 g (3½ oz) mature Cheddar
  cheese, grated
1½ tablespoons chopped chives
1 small egg, lightly beaten
salt and pepper
salad leaves, to serve (optional)

- Line a baking sheet with baking paper.

- Melt the butter in a large frying pan and cook the leeks for 4–5 minutes, until softened.

- Meanwhile, roll out the pastry on a lightly floured work surface and stamp out 4 x 22 cm (8½ inch) circles.

- Transfer the leeks to a large bowl, add the tuna, potato, cheese, chives and a pinch of salt and pepper and mix well.

- Spoon the mixture into the middle of each pastry circle, then brush a little beaten egg around the border. Fold up the pastry, pinching and crimping the edges together along the top to encase the filling.

- Arrange the pasties on the prepared baking sheet, brush with beaten egg and bake in a preheated oven, 220°C (425°F), Gas Mark 7, for about 15 minutes, or until puffed and golden. Cool slightly and serve with salad leaves, if desired.

 Quick Tuna and Chive Toasties

Place the tuna, cheese and chives from the main recipe in a bowl. Add 4 tablespoons mayonnaise and 1 teaspoon lemon juice, season and mix well. Spread thickly over 4 slices of country-style bread. Place a small handful of baby spinach or rocket leaves on each, then top with another slice of bread. Toast in a dry frying pan for 3–4 minutes, turning once. Alternatively, toast in a panini machine following the manufacturer's instructions, until melting and golden.

 Quick Tuna and Chive Rissoles

Cook the leeks in the melted butter, as in the main recipe. Meanwhile, place 75 g (3 oz) cooked rice, 50 g (2 oz) freshly made breadcrumbs and 1 large beaten egg in a bowl or food processor. Add the tuna, cheese and chives from the main recipe, then the softened leek, and stir or pulse briefly to combine. Shape into about 12 rissoles and dust lightly in plain flour, shaking off the excess. Heat 3 tablespoons olive oil in a large frying pan over a medium heat

and cook the rissoles for 3–5 minutes, turning once, until crisp and golden. Serve with tartare sauce and salad leaves, if desired.

10 Fillet Steak Bourguignon

Serves 2

3 tablespoons olive oil

100 g (3½ oz) lardons

75 g (3 oz) portobellini or small field mushrooms, sliced

2 fillet steaks

100 ml (3½ fl oz) red wine

125 ml (4 fl oz) good-quality beef stock

25 g (1 oz) cold butter, diced

salt and pepper

mashed potato, to serve

- Heat half the olive oil in a large frying pan and cook the lardons over a medium-high heat for 2–3 minutes, until golden. Add the mushrooms and cook for a further 2–3 minutes, until softened and golden.

- Meanwhile, heat the remaining oil in a separate pan and cook the steaks over a medium-high heat for 2–3 minutes on each side, or until cooked to your liking. Transfer to a plate and keep warm.

- Pour the wine into the empty pan and stir over a medium-low heat, scraping up any bits stuck to the bottom, until the wine becomes syrupy. Add to the bacon mixture, then pour in the stock and simmer hard to reduce by half. Season to taste, then gradually whisk in the butter until the sauce is smooth and glossy.

- Arrange the steaks on warmed plates and serve immediately with the bourguignon sauce and hot mashed potato.

20 Cheat's Boeuf Bourguignon

Heat 2 tablespoons olive oil in a frying pan and add 300 g (10 oz) sirloin steak cut into thick strips. Cook over a high heat for 3–4 minutes, until browned. Transfer to a plate and set aside. Return the pan to a medium-high heat and cook 100 g (3½ oz) cubed pancetta for 2–3 minutes, until golden. Add 4 quartered small shallots, fry for 3–4 minutes, until golden, then add 100 g (3½ oz) halved baby button mushrooms and fry for a further 2–3 minutes. Pour in 2 tablespoons brandy and 125 ml (4 fl oz) red wine and heat until reduced and syrupy. Add 125 ml (4 fl oz) beef stock and simmer to reduce by half. Return the meat to the pan, heat through and serve with hot mashed potato.

30 Burgundy-Style Beef Pies

Make the boeuf bourguignon as in the 20-minute recipe, then spoon into 2 individual pie dishes. Meanwhile, chop 500 g (1 lb) potatoes into chunks and cook in a pan of salted boiling water for 12–15 minutes. Drain and return to the pan with 50 g (2 oz) butter and a pinch of nutmeg, salt and pepper. Mash until smooth, then spoon over the pie filling and sprinkle with 3 tablespoons grated Cheddar cheese. Slide under a preheated medium-hot grill for 6–7 minutes, until golden.

20 Grilled Tortellini with Cheese and Bacon

Serves 4

800 g (1 lb 10 oz) fresh tortellini, such as tomato and basil

2 tablespoons olive oil

200 g (7 oz) bacon, diced

150 g (5 oz) mushrooms, sliced (optional)

400 g (13 oz) half-fat crème fraîche

75 g (3 oz) blue cheese, such as Stilton or Roquefort, crumbled

black pepper

100 g (3½ oz) Cheddar cheese, grated

green salad, to serve (optional)

- Cook the pasta in a large pan of lightly salted boiling water for 2–3 minutes, or according to the packet instructions, until tender. Drain, reserving 3 tablespoons of the cooking water, then tip the tortellini into 1 large or 4 individual ovenproof dishes.

- Meanwhile, heat the oil in a frying pan and cook the bacon over a medium heat for 4–5 minutes, until browned. Add the mushrooms and cook for a further 3–4 minutes, until golden.

- Stir in the crème fraîche and reserved cooking water, the blue cheese and a pinch of black pepper. Heat gently until the cheese has melted, then pour the mixture over the pasta.

- Sprinkle with the Cheddar and slide the dish(es) under a preheated medium-hot grill for 6–7 minutes, or until bubbling and golden. Serve with a green salad, if desired.

---

10 Cheesy Penne with Crispy Bacon

Grill 8 streaky bacon rashers under a preheated medium-hot grill for 6–7 minutes. Cook 700 g (1 lb 7 oz) fresh penne pasta in a pan of salted boiling water for 2–3 minutes. Drain and return to the pan with 2 tablespoons of the cooking water. Meanwhile, melt 25 g (1 oz) butter in a frying pan and cook 150 g (5 oz) mushrooms for 3–4 minutes. Stir in the crème fraîche, blue cheese and black pepper from the main recipe. When the cheese has melted, stir the mixture into the pasta. Crumble the crispy bacon over the top and serve immediately.

30 Crunchy-Topped Macaroni Cheese

Cook 350 g (11½ oz) macaroni or other pasta tubes in a large pan of lightly salted boiling water for 10 minutes, or according to the packet instructions, until 'al dente'. Meanwhile, cook the bacon and mushrooms following the main recipe. Place 600 ml (1 pint) milk in a saucepan with 75 g (3 oz) plain flour and 75 g (3 oz) butter and bring slowly to the boil, stirring constantly with a balloon whisk, until thick and smooth. Simmer for 1–2 minutes, then season lightly. Take off the heat and stir in 100 g (3½ oz) crumbled blue cheese and season with plenty of black pepper. Mix with the drained pasta, bacon and mushrooms, then place in a large, ovenproof dish. Top with 2 tablespoons grated Parmesan cheese and 2 tablespoons fresh breadcrumbs and bake in a preheated oven, 220°C (425°F), Gas Mark 7, for about 15 minutes, until the top is golden and crunchy.

30 Chicken and Winter Vegetable Tray-Roast

Serves 4

4 tablespoons olive oil
4 chicken breasts, skin on
400 g (13 oz) small waxy potatoes, halved
400 g (13 oz) carrots, quartered
400 g (13 oz) parsnips, cored and quartered
4 banana shallots, quartered
6 small garlic cloves
2 thyme sprigs
rosemary sprig
salt and pepper
steamed kale, to serve (optional)

- Heat half the oil in a large frying pan over a medium-high heat and cook the chicken, skin-side down without moving, for 7–8 minutes, until the skin is really crisp and golden.

- Meanwhile, parboil the potatoes in a large pan of salted boiling water for 6–7 minutes, adding the carrots and parsnips for the final 3 minutes. They should all be starting to soften.

- Drain well and place in a large roasting tin. Add the shallots, garlic, herbs and remaining oil, season generously and toss well. Nestle the chicken in with the vegetables, skin-side up.

- Roast in a preheated oven, 220°C (425°F), Gas Mark 7, for about 20 minutes, until the chicken is cooked and the vegetables are golden. Serve with steamed kale, if desired.

10 Hearty Roast Chicken Salad

Heat 2 tablespoons olive oil in a frying pan and cook 200 g (7 oz) smoked lardons or chopped pancetta over a medium-high heat for 3–4 minutes, until golden. Transfer to a plate and keep hot. Add 400 g (13 oz) sliced, cooked new potatoes and cook for 4–5 minutes, turning occasionally, until lightly golden. Meanwhile, remove the meat from 1 small roast chicken or 4 roast chicken legs in large pieces and arrange on serving plates with 150 g (5 oz) winter salad leaves. Scatter the bacon and potatoes over the top and serve immediately with your preferred dressing.

20 Pan-Fried Chicken with Roasted Vegetables

Vegetables Tip a 480 g (15¼ oz) bag winter vegetable mix, such as sprouts, carrots and broccoli, into a large roasting tin with 500 g (1 lb) halved miniature new potatoes. Toss with 3 tablespoons olive oil, 2 thyme sprigs and a generous pinch of salt and pepper. Roast in a preheated oven, 230°C (450°F), Gas Mark 8, for 18 minutes, shaking the pan occasionally, until tender and golden. Meanwhile, heat 2 tablespoons olive oil in a large frying pan and cook 4 seasoned chicken breasts, skin-side down, for 8–10 minutes, until really golden. Turn the chicken and cook for a further 3–5 minutes, or until the juices run clear. Serve the chicken with roasted vegetables.

WIN-COMF-ZUF

30 Comforting Fish Pie

Serves 4

750 g (1½ lb) floury potatoes, cut into chunks
2 eggs (optional)
400 ml (14 fl oz) full-fat milk
50 g (2 oz) plain flour
100 g (3½ oz) butter
2 tablespoons chopped parsley
25 g (1 oz) watercress, roughly chopped (optional)
390 g (12¾ oz) shop-bought fish pie mixture (available from the chilled section of supermarkets), or use bite-sized chunks of salmon, white fish fillet and smoked haddock
200 g (7 oz) raw peeled king prawns
3 tablespoons crème fraîche
75 g (3 oz) Cheddar cheese, grated
green salad, to serve
salt and pepper

- Cook the potatoes in a pan of lightly salted boiling water for 10–12 minutes, until tender.

- Hard-boil the eggs, if using, in a pan of simmering water for about 8 minutes. Drain and hold under cold running water. Once cool enough to handle, remove the shells and cut the eggs into wedges.

- Place the milk, flour and half the butter in a saucepan and bring slowly to the boil, stirring constantly with a balloon whisk, until thick and smooth. Simmer for 1–2 minutes, then season lightly and take off the heat.

- Stir the parsley, watercress (if using), fish, prawns and egg into the sauce, then transfer to an ovenproof dish.

- Drain the potatoes and mash them with the crème fraîche and the remaining butter. Season to taste, then spoon over the fish mixture and scatter with the grated cheese. Place the pie in a preheated oven, 220°C (425°F), Gas Mark 7, for 12–15 minutes, until golden and bubbling and the fish is cooked. Serve with green salad.

 Creamy Fish with Mashed Potatoes

Heat 1 kg (2 lb) shop-bought mashed potatoes according to the packet instructions. Melt 50 g (2 oz) butter in a frying pan and cook 4 seasoned white fish fillets over a medium-low heat for 5–7 minutes, turning once, until flaky. Pour in 200 g (7 oz) shop-bought watercress sauce and heat for 1–2 minutes, then serve with the mashed potatoes and a watercress salad.

Cheat's Fish Gratin

Pour a 230 g (7½ oz) pack fish pie sauce into a saucepan with the fish mixture and king prawns used in the main recipe. Warm gently until boiling, then simmer for 2–3 minutes, until the fish is just cooked. Transfer to an ovenproof dish. Top with 500 g (1 lb) cooked sliced potatoes, dot with 50 g (2 oz) butter and sprinkle with 75 g (3 oz) grated mature Cheddar. Slide under a preheated medium-hot grill for 7–8 minutes, until golden and bubbling. Serve with a watercress salad.

WIN-COMF-TAT

20 Sun-Dried Tomato and Mascarpone Grilled Gnocchi

Serves 2

50 g (2 oz) sun-dried tomatoes, drained and chopped

50 g (2 oz) roasted red peppers, drained

3 tablespoons freshly grated Parmesan cheese

125 g (4 oz) mascarpone cheese

1 tablespoon chopped basil

400 g (13 oz) gnocchi

salt and pepper

rocket and Parmesan salad, to serve (optional)

- Place the tomatoes and peppers in a blender or food processor and whizz to a chunky paste. Transfer to a bowl and beat in 1 tablespoon of the Parmesan, the mascarpone, basil and a pinch of salt and pepper.

- Cook the gnocchi in a large pan of salted boiling water for 1–3 minutes, or according to the packet instructions, until they float to the surface. Drain and tip into 1 medium or 2 individual ovenproof dishes.

- Spoon the mascarpone mixture evenly over the gnocchi, sprinkle with the remaining Parmesan and slide under a preheated medium-hot grill for 6–8 minutes, until bubbling and golden. Cool slightly before serving with a rocket and Parmesan salad, if desired.

10 Sun-Dried Tomato and Gnocchi Salad

Bowl Heat 1 tablespoon olive oil in a large frying pan and fry 400 g (13 oz) fresh potato gnocchi for 6–7 minutes, tossing frequently, until crisp and golden. Meanwhile, gently combine 75 g (3 oz) rocket and watercress leaves with the sun-dried tomatoes, roasted peppers and basil from the main recipe. Heap into 2 pasta bowls and top with the gnocchi. Scatter each serving with a small handful of Parmesan shavings, plus a drizzle of olive oil and balsamic glaze.

30 Sun-Dried Tomato and Mascarpone

Bake Heat 1 tablespoon olive oil in a frying pan and cook 2 chopped shallots and 1 chopped garlic clove over a medium heat for 3–4 minutes, until beginning to soften. Stir in a 400 g (13 oz) can cherry tomatoes, 100 g (3½ oz) chopped sun-dried tomatoes and 100 g (3½ oz) roasted red peppers. Simmer for 5–6 minutes, until thickened slightly, then stir in 125 g (4 oz) mascarpone. Add 400 g (13 oz) fresh gnocchi and 1 tablespoon chopped basil, bring to the boil and season to taste. Transfer to an ovenproof dish and sprinkle 2 tablespoons freshly grated Parmesan over the top. Bake in a preheated oven, 200°C (400°F), Gas Mark 6, for about 15 minutes, until bubbling and golden. Serve as above.

10 Cheese and Onion Rarebit

Serves 4

6 tablespoons caramelized onion or onion chutney

4 large slices of sourdough bread, lightly toasted

150 g (5 oz) shop-bought four-cheese sauce

150 g (5 oz) mature Cheddar cheese, grated

2 tablespoons wholegrain mustard

2 egg yolks

salt and pepper

To serve

Worcestershire sauce (optional)

green salad

- Spread the chutney over the toasted bread.

- Put all the remaining ingredients into a bowl and beat together. Season to taste and spread over the toasts.

- Place under a preheated medium-hot grill for 4–6 minutes, or until the topping is melting and golden. Serve with Worcestershire sauce, if desired, and a green salad.

---

20 Cheese and Onion Pizza

Mix 1 tablespoon wholegrain mustard with 150 g (5 oz) shop-bought four-cheese sauce and 2 tablespoons caramelized onions. Spread thinly over 2 large, shop-bought pizza bases. Top with 1 small, thinly sliced red onion and 75 g (3 oz) pitted black olives. Place in a preheated oven, 200°C (400°F), Gas Mark 6, for 12–15 minutes, until crisp. Serve with a salad, as above.

30 Cheese, Potato and Onion

Turnovers Melt 25 g (1 oz) butter in a large frying pan with 1 tablespoon olive oil. Cook 1 thinly sliced onion over a medium heat for 6–7 minutes, until softened. Meanwhile, unroll a 375 g (12 oz) sheet of puff pastry and cut into 4 equal rectangles. Dice 150 g (5 oz) cooked potatoes and place in a bowl with 125 g (4 oz) coarsely grated mature Cheddar, 75 g (3 oz) crumbled Stilton, 1 tablespoon wholegrain mustard, 2 tablespoons chopped parsley and a generous pinch of black pepper. Add the softened onion and mix well. Divide the mixture between the pastry rectangles, then brush the border with a little beaten egg and fold the pastry over the filling, pinching the edges to seal. Brush the top with beaten egg, place on a baking sheet lined with baking paper and bake in a preheated oven, 220°C (425°F), Gas Mark 7, for 15–18 minutes, until puffed up and golden.

30 Cajun-Spiced Turkey Meatballs

Serves 4

1 kg (2 lb) sweet potatoes,
   cut into thin wedges
4 tablespoons vegetable oil
1 small red onion, sliced
1 red pepper, deseeded and sliced
2 garlic cloves
4 teaspoons Cajun-style
   spice blend
680 g (1 lb 6 oz) jar passata
pinch of sugar
salt and pepper
soured cream, to serve (optional)

For the meatballs

500 g (1 lb) minced turkey
2 teaspoons Cajun-style spice
   blend
2 spring onions, finely chopped
50 g (2 oz) fresh breadcrumbs
2 tablespoons chopped coriander

- Place the sweet potatoes in a roasting tin with half the oil and season. Toss well, then roast in a preheated oven, 220°C (425°F), Gas Mark 7, for 20–25 minutes, until golden and tender.

- Meanwhile, combine all the meatball ingredients in a bowl, adding some salt and pepper. Roll into 20–24 balls. Heat the remaining oil in a large pan and cook the meatballs over a medium-high heat for 3–4 minutes, shaking the pan occasionally, until browned. Transfer to a plate and set aside.

- Return the oily pan to the heat and cook the onion, pepper and garlic for 7–8 minutes, until softened and lightly coloured. Add the spice mix and stir over a medium heat for 1 minute. Pour in the passata, add a pinch of salt, pepper and sugar and simmer for 5–6 minutes to thicken slightly.

- Add the meatballs to the sauce and simmer for a further 6–7 minutes, until cooked and the sauce has thickened. Serve with the sweet potato wedges and a dollop of soured cream, if desired.

 Cajun-Spiced Turkey Burgers

Make the meatball mixture as in the main recipe, then form into 4 large burgers. Heat 2 tablespoons oil in a large frying pan and cook the burgers over a medium-high heat for 7–8 minutes, turning once, until cooked and golden. Place inside 4 warmed burger buns and serve immediately with any desired toppings, such as spicy salsa, thinly sliced red onion and red pepper.

 Cajun-Spiced Turkey Fajitas

Thinly slice 400 g (13 oz) turkey fillet steaks. Place in a bowl with 1 tablespoon Cajun-style spice and mix well to coat. Heat 2 tablespoons vegetable oil in a frying pan and stir-fry 1 sliced onion and 1 deseeded and sliced red pepper over a medium-high heat for 3–4 minutes, until lightly charred but still firm. Transfer to a plate, then return the pan to a medium-high heat and stir-fry the turkey strips for 6–7 minutes, until cooked through. Meanwhile, warm 4 large, soft flour tortillas according to the packet instructions. Return the onion and pepper to the pan and mix well. Fill the tortillas with the turkey filling, then roll up and serve immediately with spicy salsa and jalapeño peppers, if desired.

10 Creamy Chicken and Mushroom Rice

Serves 4

50 g (2 oz) butter
3 spring onions, sliced
2 roast chicken breasts, sliced
  or shredded
500 g (1 lb) shop-bought
  long-grain and wild rice mixture
290 g (9¾ oz) jar mushroom
  antipasti, drained
4 tablespoons crème fraîche
salt and pepper

- Melt the butter in a large frying pan and cook the spring onions for 2–3 minutes over a medium heat, until softened. Add the chicken, rice and all but a small handful of the mushrooms. Stir-fry for 3–4 minutes, until piping hot.

- Add the crème fraîche, season to taste and stir occasionally for about 2 minutes, until hot and creamy. Spoon into shallow bowls and serve immediately, topped with the reserved mushrooms.

20 Chicken and Mushroom Fried Rice

Cook 350 g (11½ oz) quick-cook long-grain rice for 8–9 minutes, or according to the packet instructions, until just tender. Drain well. Heat 2 tablespoons vegetable oil in a large frying pan or wok and fry 3 sliced spring onions with 2 chopped garlic cloves for 2–3 minutes. Add 200 g (7 oz) diced chestnut mushrooms and the shredded chicken from the main recipe and stir-fry for 3–4 minutes, until soft and golden. Increase the heat slightly and add the rice plus 75 g (3 oz) defrosted peas. Stir-fry for 3–4 minutes, until hot and lightly golden. Season to taste, then spoon into bowls and serve with soy sauce.

30 Chicken and Wild Mushroom Risotto

Place 15 g (½ oz) dried mushrooms in a saucepan with 1.2 litres (2 pints) chicken stock, then cover and simmer for about 10 minutes. Meanwhile, melt 50 g (2 oz) butter in a frying pan and cook 1 finely chopped onion and 2 chopped garlic cloves for 5–6 minutes, until softened. Add 200 g (7 oz) diced chestnut mushrooms and cook for a further 2–3 minutes, until softened. Add 350 g (11½ oz) risotto rice and stir until the grains are coated and translucent. Pour in 125 ml (4 fl oz) dry vermouth or dry white wine and simmer rapidly, stirring constantly, until it has been absorbed. Drain the dried mushrooms, returning the stock to the pan and keeping it hot. Add the stock to the rice a ladleful at a time, stirring constantly at a gentle simmer until each ladleful has been absorbed. Continue until all of the stock has been used and the rice is 'al dente'. This should take about 17 minutes. Roughly chop the dried mushrooms and stir into the rice. Serve with grated Parmesan, if desired.

WIN-COMF-ZEQ

3⟨ Deep-Pan Meat-Feast Pizza

Serves 2

200 g (7 oz) self-raising flour
1 teaspoon baking powder
½ teaspoon salt
½ teaspoon ground black pepper
1 teaspoon dried oregano
2 small eggs, lightly beaten
4 tablespoons sun-dried
   tomato purée
1 tablespoon olive oil
3–4 tablespoons milk
150 g (5 oz) thinly sliced meats,
   such as salami, prosciutto and
   garlic sausage
125 g (4 oz) mozzarella cheese,
   thinly sliced
50 g (2 oz) mixed pitted olives
   (optional)
chilli oil, to drizzle (optional)
mixed salad, to serve (optional)

- Sift the flour and baking powder into a bowl, then add the salt, pepper and oregano.

- Add the eggs, half the tomato purée, the olive oil and enough milk to create a soft dough. Flatten into 1 or 2 circles about 1 cm (½ inch) thick and place on a baking sheet.

- Spread the remaining tomato purée over the pizza base(s) and top them with the sliced meats, mozzarella and olives. Bake in a preheated oven, 200°C (400°F), Gas Mark 6, for 10–15 minutes, until the base is crisp and the topping melted. Cut into wedges, drizzle with chilli oil, if desired, and serve with a mixed salad, if liked.

 Meat-Feast Pitta Pizza

Spread 2 tablespoons sun-dried tomato purée or pizza sauce over 2 large pitta breads. Top with the mozzarella, sliced meats and olives from the main recipe. Arrange on baking sheets and place in a preheated oven, 200°C (400°F), Gas Mark 6, for 5–7 minutes, until crisp and melting. Serve as above.

 Frying-Pan Meat-Feast Pizza

Mix 150 g (5 oz) plain flour in a bowl with ½ teaspoon dried oregano and a generous pinch of salt and pepper. Pour in 75 ml (3 fl oz) warm water and 2 teaspoons olive oil and knead to form a smooth dough. Roll out to fit a large frying pan and dust with a little flour. Heat the frying pan over a medium heat. When hot, add the dough and cook for about 10 minutes, turning once, until lightly golden. Spread 2 tablespoons pizza sauce over the pizza base and scatter with the mozzarella, meats and olives from the main recipe. Place under a preheated, medium-hot grill for 3–5 minutes, until golden and bubbling, then serve as above.

20 Quick-Fried Steak Stroganoff

Serves 2

25 g (1 oz) butter

1½ tablespoons olive oil

2 shallots, finely chopped

150 g (5 oz) chestnut
   mushrooms, sliced

2 teaspoons sweet paprika

150 ml (¼ pint) soured cream

1 teaspoon rinsed and drained
   green peppercorns

2 sirloin steaks

1–2 tablespoons chopped parsley

salt and pepper

shop-bought long-grain and wild
   rice mixture, to serve

- Melt the butter in a frying pan with 1 tablespoon of the oil and cook the shallots over a medium heat for 3–4 minutes, until softened. Add the mushrooms and fry for 3–4 minutes, until soft and golden.

- Sprinkle in the paprika and heat for 1 minute, then stir in the soured cream and peppercorns. Season to taste and simmer for 2–3 minutes, until thickened slightly.

- Meanwhile, heat the remaining oil in a large frying pan and cook the steaks for 4–8 minutes, turning once, until done to your liking. Set aside to rest for 2–3 minutes, adding any juices to the stroganoff sauce.

- Arrange the steaks on serving plates and serve with the sauce, parsley and cooked rice.

10 Stripped Beef and Mushroom Pan-Fry

Heat 2 tablespoons olive oil in a large frying pan and cook 250 g (8 oz) thinly sliced beef strips over a high heat for 2–3 minutes, until browned. Transfer to a plate and set aside. Place 150 g (5 oz) sliced mushrooms in the pan with 25 g (1 oz) butter and 1 chopped garlic clove and fry for 2–3 minutes, until soft and golden. Sprinkle 2 teaspoons sweet paprika over the top and stir for 1 minute. Add 150 ml (¼ pint) soured cream, simmer for 1 minute and season to taste. Return the beef to the pan to reheat. Serve with the rice and parsley, as above.

30 Lazy Beef and Mushroom

Stroganoff Heat 2 tablespoons oil in a large frying pan and cook 250 g (8 oz) sliced sirloin over a high heat for 3–4 minutes, until browned. Transfer to a plate and set aside. Place 25 g (1 oz) butter in the pan and cook 1 finely chopped onion and 1 deseeded and sliced green pepper for 5–6 minutes, until softened slightly. Add 150 g (5 oz) halved baby button mushrooms with 1 chopped garlic clove and cook for 3–4 minutes, until soft and golden. Stir 2 teaspoons sweet paprika and 2 teaspoons plain flour into the pan, cook for 1 minute, then add 3 tablespoons dry sherry and simmer until completely evaporated. Pour in 150 ml (¼ pint) good-quality beef stock and simmer to reduce by half. Add 150 ml (¼ pint) soured cream, a generous pinch of salt and pepper and 2 tablespoons chopped parsley. Bring to the boil, then return the beef to the pan and simmer for 2–3 minutes, until hot and tender. Serve with the rice and parsley, as above.

WIN-COMF-BUX

20 Cacciatore-Style Chicken and Salami Pasta

Serves 4

3 tablespoons olive oil
1 red onion, thinly sliced
2 garlic cloves, chopped
400 g (13 oz) chicken breast, thinly sliced
90 g (3¼ oz) salami, thinly sliced and halved
125 ml (4 fl oz) red wine
2 rosemary sprigs, leaves chopped
2 x 400 g (13 oz) cans cherry tomatoes
75 g (3 oz) green olives (optional)
400 g (13 oz) pasta, such as fusilli
salt and pepper

- Heat the oil in a large frying pan and cook the onion and garlic over a medium-high heat for 4–5 minutes, until slightly softened. Add the chicken and salami and cook for a further 3–4 minutes, until lightly golden.

- Pour the wine into the pan and simmer until completely evaporated. Add the rosemary, tomatoes and olives (if using) and simmer for 8–10 minutes, until thickened slightly. Season to taste.

- Meanwhile, cook the pasta in a large pan of lightly salted boiling water for about 11 minutes, or according to the packet instructions, until 'al dente'. Drain and heap into serving bowls. Top with the sauce and serve.

10 Cacciatore Chicken and Salami Ciabatta

Heat 2 tablespoons olive oil in a frying pan and fry 400 g (13 oz) mini chicken fillets over a medium-high heat for 8 minutes, turning occasionally, or until cooked through and golden. Transfer to a plate and set aside. Meanwhile, cut 1 large ciabatta loaf into 8 sandwich slices. Divide 90 g (3¼ oz) sliced salami between 4 pieces of the bread. Slice 150 g (5 oz) cherry tomatoes, 50 g (2 oz) green olives and half a small red onion. Put a little of each on top of the salami, then add some of the chicken fillets and a small handful of rocket. Cover with the remaining bread and serve.

30 Oven-Baked Chicken and Salami Cacciatore

Prepare the cacciatore sauce following the main recipe, but omitting the chicken, salami and olives. Bring to the boil and simmer for 4–5 minutes, until thickened slightly. Meanwhile, place 4 skinless, boneless chicken breasts between 2 pieces of clingfilm and bash with a rolling pin to flatten slightly. Heat 2 tablespoons olive oil in a large frying pan and cook the chicken over a medium-high heat for 5–6 minutes, turning once, until golden. Transfer to a large ovenproof dish with the salami and olives from the main recipe. Pour over the sauce and bake in a preheated oven, 220°C (425°F), Gas Mark 7, for about 15 minutes, until the chicken is cooked through. Serve with cooked pasta, as in the main recipe.

10 Quick Fish Schnitzel with Tartare Sauce

Serves 2

50 g (2 oz) breadcrumbs
1 tablespoon dried parsley
½ teaspoon grated lemon rind
1 egg
2 tablespoons plain flour
2 thin white fish fillets, such as plaice or haddock
3 tablespoons olive oil
salt and pepper

To serve

tartare sauce
lemon wedges
cooked garden peas

- Mix the breadcrumbs, parsley and lemon rind in a shallow dish. Break the egg into a second dish and beat lightly. Place the flour in a third dish, add some seasoning and mix well.

- Dip the fish fillets first in the seasoned flour, then the egg, followed by the breadcrumbs, ensuring each is well coated.

- Heat the oil in a large frying pan and cook the fish over a medium heat for 2–3 minutes on each side, until golden and flaky. Drain on kitchen paper and serve with tartare sauce, lemon wedges and peas.

 Baskets of Fish Goujons with Lemon Cut 2 chunky fish fillets into strips and coat with the flour, egg and breadcrumbs, as above. Arrange on a baking sheet lined with baking paper and place in a preheated oven, 200°C (400°F), Gas Mark 6, for about 15 minutes, or until golden and flaky. Pile the goujons into baskets with oven chips and serve with lemon wedges and tartare sauce, as above.

 Staying-In Fish and Chips Cut 400 g (13 oz) waxy potatoes into chips and place in a nonstick roasting tin. Add 2 tablespoons olive oil and a pinch of salt and pepper and toss well. Roast in a preheated oven, 220°C (425°F), Gas Mark 7, for 20–25 minutes, until tender and golden. Meanwhile, coat 2 chunky white fish fillets or loins in flour, egg and breadcrumbs following the main recipe. Heat a nonstick frying pan over a medium heat and shallow-fry the fish for 7–8 minutes, turning once, until golden and flaky. Drain on kitchen paper, then arrange on plates with the homemade chips and serve with tartare sauce and lemon wedges, as above.

3⦿ Cheat's Creamy Ham and Ricotta Cannelloni

Serves 4

3 tablespoons olive oil

2 garlic cloves, chopped

2 x 400 g (13 oz) cans chopped tomatoes

2 tablespoons sun-dried tomato purée

pinch of sugar

2 tablespoons chopped basil

250 g (8 oz) ricotta cheese

150 g (5 oz) diced ham

290 g (9½ oz) jar wild mushroom antipasto, drained

½ teaspoon grated lemon rind

250 g (8 oz) fresh lasagne sheets, halved widthways

125 g (4 oz) grated Cheddar cheese

salt and pepper

- Heat the oil in a large frying pan and cook the garlic over a medium heat for 1 minute, to soften. Add the tomatoes, tomato purée, sugar, basil and a generous pinch of salt and pepper and simmer for 5–7 minutes, to thicken slightly.

- Meanwhile, place the ricotta in a pan with the ham, mushrooms and lemon rind and heat gently until warm but not hot. Divide the mixture between the halved lasagne sheets and roll up to form filled tubes.

- Pour half the tomato sauce into an ovenproof dish, arrange the cannelloni in it, then cover with the remaining sauce. Sprinkle with the grated cheese and bake in a preheated oven, 220°C (425°F), Gas Mark 7, for about 20 minutes, until the top is bubbling and golden and the lasagne tender.

1⦿ Creamy Ham and Ricotta Pancakes

Put 250 g (8 oz) ricotta in a pan with 150 g (5 oz) pulled or diced ham, 200 g (7 oz) creamed mushrooms and 1 tablespoon chopped basil and season. Stir over a medium heat until hot. Spoon the mixture on to 8 shop-bought plain pancakes, then fold in half and arrange in a large ovenproof dish. Scatter 100 g (3½ oz) grated Cheddar over the top, then slide under a preheated medium-hot grill for 2–3 minutes, until melted. Serve with crusty bread and a green salad.

2⦿ Creamy Ham and Ricotta Penne

Cook 400 g (13 oz) penne pasta in a large pan of salted boiling water for 11 minutes, or according to the packet instructions, until 'al dente'. Drain, reserving 2 tablespoons of the cooking water. Meanwhile, melt 50 g (2 oz) butter in a large frying pan and cook 3 chopped banana shallots and 2 chopped garlic cloves for 3–4 minutes, until softened. Add 200 g (7 oz) sliced mushrooms and cook for a further 3–4 minutes, until soft and golden. Stir in 150 g (5 oz) chopped ham, 250 g (8 oz) ricotta, 150 ml (¼ pint) single cream, 1 teaspoon lemon juice and 2 tablespoons chopped basil. Season to taste, bring to boiling point, then stir into the drained pasta with the reserved water. Spoon into warmed bowls to serve.

10 Cottage Pie Waffles

Serves 4

2 tablespoons olive oil

1 onion, chopped

2 carrots, finely diced

100 g (3½ oz) frozen peas

1 tablespoon tomato purée

250 g (8 oz) piece of rare roast beef, diced

300 g (10 oz) good-quality roast beef stock

2 teaspoons Worcestershire sauce

1 teaspoon thyme leaves (optional)

8 grilled potato waffles, to serve

- Heat the olive oil in a large pan and cook the onion over a medium-high heat for 5–6 minutes, until softened.

- Meanwhile, cook the carrots in a pan of lightly salted boiling water for 5–6 minutes, until just tender, adding the peas for the final 2 minutes. Drain.

- Add the tomato purée to the onions and stir for 1 minute. Mix in the beef, stock, Worcestershire sauce and thyme (if using). Stir in the carrots and peas, then simmer for 2 minutes, until thickened slightly. Spoon over the grilled waffles to serve.

 Superfast Cottage Pies

Make the cottage pie filling following the main recipe, adding a 400 g (13 oz) can rinsed and drained haricot beans. Meanwhile, heat 1 kg (2 lb) shop-bought cheesy mashed potato according to the packet instructions. Spoon the filling into 4 individual ovenproof pie dishes and top with the mash. Slide under a preheated medium-hot grill for 6–7 minutes, until bubbling and golden.

 Cottage Pie with Cheesy Parsnip Mash

Place 350 g (11½ oz) diced parsnips and 350 g (11½ oz) diced potatoes in a large pan of lightly salted boiling water and cook for 10–12 minutes, until tender. Drain and mash with 75 g (3 oz) grated mature Double Gloucester or Cheddar cheese, 50 g (2 oz) butter and 1 tablespoon chopped chives and season. Meanwhile, heat 3 tablespoons olive oil in a large frying pan and cook 1 chopped onion, 1 chopped carrot, 1 chopped leek and 100 g (3½ oz) diced chestnut mushrooms over a medium-high heat for 7–8 minutes, until beginning to soften. Increase the heat, add 500 g (1 lb) minced beef and cook for 2–3 minutes, until browned all over. Reduce the heat and add 1 tablespoon plain flour and 2 tablespoons tomato purée, stirring for 1 minute. Pour in 300 ml (½ pint) beef stock with the Worcestershire sauce and thyme from the main recipe. Simmer for 4–5 minutes, until rich and thick. Transfer to a large ovenproof dish and top with the cheesy mash. Scatter 75 g (3 oz) grated cheese over the mash and slide under a preheated medium-hot grill for 6–8 minutes, until bubbling and golden.

30 Feta-Stuffed Chicken with Chilli and Capers

Serves 4

200 g (7 oz) feta cheese, crumbled
1 red chilli, deseeded and chopped
2 teaspoons rinsed capers
1 teaspoon grated lemon rind
70 g (2¾ oz) pitted olives, sliced
2 tablespoons chopped coriander
   or parsley
2 tablespoons olive oil
4 chicken breasts, skin on
4 lemon wedges
2 Romano peppers, halved
   lengthways and deseeded
250 g (8 oz) wholewheat
   couscous
salt and pepper

- Place the feta into a small bowl and add the chilli, capers, lemon rind, olives, coriander or parsley and half the olive oil. Season generously with salt and pepper.

- Cut a pocket into the side of each chicken breast and fill with half the feta mixture. Place skin-side up in an ovenproof dish with the lemon wedges and Romano peppers.

- Drizzle over the remaining olive oil and place in a preheated oven, 220°C (425°F), Gas Mark 7, for about 20 minutes, until the chicken is cooked and golden.

- Meanwhile, cook the couscous according to the packet instructions, fluff up with a fork and fold in the remaining feta mixture. Spoon on to plates and serve with the stuffed chicken, roasted peppers and lemon wedges.

 Chilli Chicken and Feta Rolls

Place 300 g (10 oz) cooked sliced chicken breast in a large bowl with the feta, chilli, capers, olives and coriander from the main recipe. Add 1 tablespoon olive oil, 2 teaspoons lemon juice, 70 g (2¾ oz) rocket leaves and a pinch of salt and pepper. Toss to combine, then heap on to 4 large, soft flour tortillas. Roll up the tortillas and toast them on a hot ridged griddle pan for 4–5 minutes, turning occasionally, until warm and charred. Cut in half diagonally and serve with a tabbouleh salad or steamed wholewheat couscous for a more substantial meal.

 Pan-Fried Chicken with Feta and Capers Place 4 skinless chicken breasts between 2 large sheets of clingfilm and bash with a rolling pin to flatten. Place in a large shallow dish with the chilli, coriander and lemon rind from the main recipe. Drizzle over 1 tablespoon olive oil and a pinch of salt and pepper and mix well to coat. Heat 2 tablespoons olive oil in a large frying pan and cook the chicken breasts over a medium-high heat for 7–8 minutes, turning once, until cooked and golden. Transfer to serving plates. Crumble 200 g (7 oz) feta over the chicken and sprinkle with 2 teaspoons rinsed and drained capers. Drizzle with a little extra olive oil and a squeeze of lemon juice and serve with steamed couscous.

Spicy Sausage and Salsa Butty

Serves 4

4 chorizo cooking sausages
 or similar spicy sausages,
 thickly sliced
4 ciabatta-style rolls, cut in half
salad leaves, to serve (optional)

For the salsa

12 baby plum tomatoes, quartered
1 avocado, peeled, stoned and diced
2 tablespoons chopped coriander
2 spring onions, finely sliced
2 teaspoons lemon juice
2 tablespoons olive oil
salt and pepper

- Heat a large, dry frying pan and cook the sausage pieces over a medium-high heat for 7–8 minutes, turning occasionally, until cooked and lightly golden.

- Meanwhile, combine the salsa ingredients in a bowl and season to taste.

- Heat a ridged grill pan and toast the cut side of the ciabatta rolls in it until they are nicely charred.

- Sandwich some sausage and salsa in each roll, topping the filling with a small handful of salad leaves, if desired.

2 Spicy Sausage and Salsa Hot Dogs

Cook 8 spicy sausages according to the packet instructions, until browned and cooked through. Meanwhile, heat 2 tablespoons vegetable oil in a large frying pan and cook 2 thinly sliced onions over a medium-low heat for about 15 minutes, until soft and golden, adding 1 finely chopped red chilli (deseeded if less heat required) for the final 4–5 minutes. Stir in 2 tablespoons chopped fresh coriander and 2 deseeded and diced tomatoes and season to taste. Spoon the hot onion salsa into 4 large, submarine-style bread rolls. Top with the cooked sausages and serve hot.

3 Spicy Sausage Rolls with Salsa

Place 450 g (14½ oz) skinless pork sausages in a bowl, add 1 finely chopped chilli (deseeded if less heat required), 2 finely chopped spring onions and 2 tablespoons chopped fresh coriander, then mix with your hands. Roll into 8 thin sausage shapes. Unroll a 375 g (12 oz) sheet of puff pastry and cut into 8 equal rectangles. Place 1 sausage on each piece of pastry, then roll up and cut in half to create 16 small sausage rolls. Place on a nonstick baking sheet, make 3 slashes in the top of each roll and brush with beaten egg. Bake in a preheated oven, 200°C (400°F), Gas Mark 6, for 15–18 minutes, until the sausage is cooked and the pastry is puffed and golden. Meanwhile, combine the salsa ingredients as above and serve with the sausage rolls.

20 Pesto and Meatball Tagliatelle

Serves 4

2 tablespoons olive oil

200 g (7 oz) smoked bacon, chopped

8 pork sausages (about 500 g/ 1 lb), skinned

1 red onion, finely chopped

2 garlic cloves, crushed

100 ml (3½ fl oz) red wine

500 g (1 lb) passata or sieved tomatoes

3 tablespoons red pesto

700 g (1 lb 7 oz) fresh tagliatelle

salt and pepper

freshly grated Parmesan cheese, to serve (optional)

- Heat the oil in a large frying pan and cook the bacon over a medium-high heat for 2–3 minutes, until lightly golden. Meanwhile, roll the sausagemeat into 24 balls. Add to the pan and fry for a further 2–3 minutes, shaking occasionally, until lightly browned all over.

- Add the onion and garlic and cook for 3–4 minutes, stirring occasionally, until beginning to soften. Pour in the wine and simmer rapidly for 1 minute, or until reduced by half. Stir the passata and pesto into the pan with a pinch of salt and pepper, then simmer for 7–8 minutes, until thickened slightly.

- Meanwhile, cook the tagliatelle in a pan of salted boiling water for 2–3 minutes, or according to the packet instructions, until 'al dente'. Drain and heap into 4 warmed bowls.

- Spoon the pesto meatballs over the pasta and serve immediately with plenty of grated Parmesan, if desired.

 Pesto Spaghetti Meatballs

Cook 700 g (1 lb 7 oz) fresh spaghetti in a pan of boiling water for 2–3 minutes, or according to the packet instructions. Heat 2 tablespoons oil in a frying pan and cook 1 chopped onion and 2 chopped garlic cloves over a medium heat for 5–6 minutes. Meanwhile, cut 400 g (13 oz) cooked pork meatballs in half and add to the pan with 500 g (1 lb) tomato pasta sauce and 2 tablespoons red pesto. Bring to the boil and simmer for 1–2 minutes, until the meatballs are hot. Serve with the spaghetti.

Sausage and Pesto Ragù Bake

Heat 2 tablespoons oil in a large frying pan and cook 1 finely chopped red onion and 2 chopped garlic cloves over a medium heat for 3–4 minutes, until beginning to soften. Increase the heat slightly and add 6 skinless sausages (about 400 g/13 oz total weight). Fry for a further 3–4 minutes, breaking up the sausagemeat as it cooks, until browned. Pour in 100 ml (3½ oz) red wine and simmer rapidly for 1 minute to reduce by half, then add the passata and red pesto from the main recipe. Simmer for 2–3 minutes to thicken slightly. Meanwhile, cook 375 g (12 oz) dried tagliatelle in a large pan of salted boiling water for 7–8 minutes, or according to the packet instructions, until almost 'al dente'. Drain well and place in a large ovenproof dish. Pour the sausage ragù over the pasta, then top with 125 g (4 oz) sliced mozzarella and a pinch of dried oregano. Drizzle with 2 teaspoons olive oil and bake in a preheated oven, 220°C (425°F), Gas Mark 7, for about 15 minutes, until bubbling and golden.

30 Greek-Style Lamb and Aubergine Bake

Serves 4–6

350 g (11½ oz) penne or rigatoni
3 tablespoons olive oil
1 onion, finely chopped
2 garlic cloves, chopped
500 g (1 lb) lean minced lamb
2 tablespoons tomato purée
½ teaspoon ground cinnamon
pinch of ground cloves
2 x 400 g (13 oz) cans chopped
   tomatoes
200 g (7 oz) drained char-grilled
   aubergines, roughly sliced
2 tablespoons chopped parsley
375 g (12 oz) shop-bought white
   sauce or cheese sauce
50 g (2 oz) Parmesan cheese,
   grated
salt and pepper

- Cook the pasta in a large pan of boiling salted water for 10–12 minutes, until almost 'al dente', then drain.

- Meanwhile, heat the oil in a large, deep-sided frying pan and cook the onion and garlic over a medium-high heat for 5–6 minutes, until softened. Add the lamb and cook for 2–3 minutes, stirring occasionally, until browned all over.

- Add the tomato purée and spices and stir for 1 minute. Add the tomatoes, aubergines and parsley, then season and simmer for 10 minutes, until thickened.

- Tip the lamb into a large ovenproof dish and top with the drained pasta. Drizzle over the white sauce and sprinkle with the Parmesan before sliding under a preheated medium-hot grill for 7–8 minutes, until golden and bubbling.

 Aubergine Greek Salad with Lamb

Rub 2 tablespoons oil over 8–12 lamb cutlets, then rub in a pinch of dried oregano and season. Slide under a preheated medium-hot grill for 5–7 minutes, turning once. Cut 5 tomatoes into wedges and place in a bowl. Add the aubergines from the main recipe, plus 70 g (2¾ oz) pitted olives, 200 g (7 oz) diced feta and half a small, sliced red onion. Stir, then sprinkle over ½ teaspoon dried oregano. Serve with the cutlets, drizzling them with olive oil and offering lemon wedges to squeeze over.

 Quick Lamb and Aubergine Bakes

Heat 2 tablespoons olive oil and cook 500 g (1 lb) minced lamb over a medium-high heat for 6–7 minutes, stirring frequently until browned all over. Meanwhile, cook 400 g (13 oz) quick-cook penne according to the packet instructions, until 'al dente'. Add 375 g (12 oz) shop-bought tomato and olive sauce to the lamb with 200 g (7 oz) sliced char-grilled aubergines and 150 g (5 oz) crumbled feta. Stir well to combine, then mix with the pasta. Divide between 4–6 shallow ovenproof dishes and pour over 375 g (12 oz) shop-bought cheese sauce. Top with 50 g (2 oz) grated Parmesan and slide under a preheated hot grill for 3–4 minutes, until golden.

Recipes listed by cooking time

30

20

1

 # Apple and Ginger Crumble Cakes

Makes 10

125 g (4 oz) dark soft brown sugar
150 g (5 oz) softened butter
3 eggs
15 g (½ oz) stem ginger in syrup,
   drained and finely chopped
1 teaspoon ground ginger
150 g (5 oz) plain flour
2 teaspoons baking powder
1 dessert apple, peeled, cored
   and coarsely grated
50 g (2 oz) shop-bought
   crumble mix

- Lightly grease a 12-hole muffin tin or line it with paper cases.

- Put the sugar, butter, eggs, both gingers, the flour and baking powder in a bowl and beat together. Stir in the apple.

- Spoon the batter into the prepared tin and sprinkle some crumble mixture over each muffin.

- Bake in a preheated oven, 190°C (375°F), Gas Mark 5, for 12–15 minutes, until risen and firm to the touch. Transfer to a wire rack and serve warm.

Apple and Ginger Smoothie

Pour 500 ml (17 fl oz) pressed apple juice into a large jug blender, add 15 g (½ oz) chopped stem ginger, 2 tablespoons stem ginger syrup, 2 roughly sliced bananas and 10 ice cubes. Blend until smooth and pour into a jug. Repeat to make enough to serve 6.

Apple and Ginger Muffins

Sift 250 g (8 oz) plain flour into a large bowl, with 1 teaspoon ground ginger, 1 teaspoon baking powder, 1 teaspoon bicarbonate of soda and a pinch of salt. Stir in 100 g (3½ oz) dark soft brown sugar. In a separate bowl or jug, beat 2 large eggs with 15 g (½ oz) finely chopped stem ginger, 1 tablespoon stem ginger syrup, 200 ml (7 fl oz) buttermilk, 50 g (2 oz) cool melted butter and 1 peeled, cored and grated dessert apple. Pour over the dry ingredients and mix until barely combined. Spoon into a prepared muffin tin, as in the main recipe, and sprinkle over 2 tablespoons rolled oats. Bake in a preheated oven, 180°C (350°F), Gas Mark 4, for 18–20 minutes, until risen and golden and firm to the touch. Transfer to a wire rack and serve warm.

10 Wintry Fruit Salad

Serves 4

2 blood oranges
1 dessert apple, cored and sliced
400 g (13 oz) pineapple chunks
75 g (3 oz) ready-to-eat dried
   figs, sliced
110 g (3¾ oz) pomegranate seeds
2 tablespoons spiced dark rum
   (optional)
1 tablespoon clear honey
50 g (2 oz) walnut halves, lightly
   crushed or chopped (optional)

- Place the oranges on a chopping board and slice off the peel and pith at both ends. Now cut away the rest of the peel and pith in the same way. Place the oranges on a plate (to catch the juices) and carefully slice between the membranes to cut into segments.

- Place the orange segments in a large bowl and gently combine with the other fruits, reserving a small handful of the pomegranate seeds.

- Mix the rum, if using, with the honey and add the orange juice from the plate. Drizzle over the salad, mixing gently to coat. Sprinkle in the reserved pomegranate seeds and walnuts, if using, and serve.

20 Wintry Warm Fruit Compote

Heat 450 ml (¾ pint) pressed apple juice in a large saucepan over a medium-high heat with 1 cinnamon stick and the spiced rum and honey from the main recipe. Add 400 g (13 oz) mixed, ready-to-eat dried fruits, such as figs, prunes, apricots and raisins. Bring to the boil, then simmer for about 12 minutes, until the fruits have plumped up. Allow to cool slightly, then spoon into bowls to serve. Alternatively, chill and serve cold with Greek yogurt.

30 Wintry Baked Fruits

Peel 2 blood oranges as in the main recipe, then slice thickly. Arrange in a large roasting tin with 6 halved and stoned plums, 2 quartered pears and 75 g (3 oz) ready-to-eat figs. Combine 2 tablespoons spiced dark rum and 2 tablespoons clear honey with 1 small cinnamon stick and 150 ml (¼ pint) pressed apple juice. Pour over the fruits and bake in a preheated oven, 200°C (400°F), Gas Mark 6, for 20–25 minutes, until tender. Spoon into shallow bowls and serve warm with Greek yogurt or crème fraîche, if desired.

30 Panettone and Butter Pudding with Raspberries

Serves 4

50 g (2 oz) softened butter
250 g (8 oz) panettone, cut into
  1.5 cm (¾ inch) slices
100 g (3½ oz) frozen raspberries
500 ml (17 fl oz) milk
3 eggs, beaten
50 g (2 oz) caster sugar
1 teaspoon vanilla bean paste
sifted icing sugar, for dusting
thick pouring cream, to serve
  (optional)

- Spread the butter over one side of each panettone slice and arrange, overlapping slightly, in a shallow, buttered ovenproof dish. Crumble or sprinkle the raspberries over the top.

- Pour the milk into a saucepan and heat until almost boiling. Meanwhile, whisk the eggs, sugar and vanilla paste together in a large bowl.

- Pour the hot milk into the egg mixture, whisking constantly, then pour over the panettone and bake in a preheated oven, 180°C (350°F), Gas Mark 4, for about 20 minutes, until just set and lightly golden. Dust with icing sugar and serve with thick pouring cream, if desired.

10 Griddled Panettone with Raspberries

Spread 75 g (3 oz) softened butter over both sides of 8 thick slices of panettone. Heat a large ridged griddle pan and toast 4 slices of panettone over a medium heat for 2–3 minutes, turning once, until striped and golden. Remove and repeat with the remaining slices. Arrange on serving plates scattered with a handful of raspberries and serve immediately, drizzled with crème anglaise, if desired.

20 Panettone and Raspberry Winter Pudding

Griddle the slices of panettone as in the 10-minute recipe. Arrange in serving dishes and dust generously with icing sugar. Meanwhile, tip 400 g (13 oz) frozen raspberries into a large pan with 3 tablespoons caster sugar and 2 tablespoons crème de cassis. Warm gently over a medium-low heat, stirring occasionally until the raspberries begin to collapse and the sugar has dissolved. Remove from the heat and allow to cool slightly. Spoon over the griddled panettone and serve with thick pouring cream, if desired.

20 Luscious Prune and Coffee Cupcakes

Serves 10

2 tablespoons cocoa powder
2 tablespoons boiling water
1½ teaspoons coffee essence
150 g (5 oz) melted butter, cooled
2 large eggs, beaten
125 g (4 oz) soft light brown sugar
75 g (3 oz) stoned prunes, finely
   chopped
125 g (4 oz) self-raising flour
whipped cream, to serve
   (optional)

- Lightly grease a 12-hole muffin tin or line it with paper cases.

- Place the cocoa powder in a large bowl, pour in the boiling water and coffee essence and stir until smooth. Add the melted butter and stir well.

- Whisk the eggs and sugar into the cocoa mixture, then add the prunes and sift in the flour. Gently fold together.

- Spoon the mixture carefully into the prepared muffin tin and bake in a preheated oven, 190°C (375°F), Gas Mark 5, for 10–12 minutes, until risen and firm to the touch. Transfer to a wire rack and serve warm or cold with whipped cream, if desired.

 Espresso Prune Purée with Greek Yogurt Pour 50 ml (2 fl oz) freshly made espresso-style coffee into a blender or food processor and add a 420 g (13¾ oz) can drained and roughly chopped prunes in light syrup. Whizz until smooth and sweeten to taste with icing sugar or honey. Spoon over bowls of Greek yogurt and serve drizzled with extra honey, if desired.

 Prune and Espresso Tiramisu Cut 6 chocolate-covered mini rolls into thick slices. Arrange in the bottom of 6 attractive serving dishes, then drizzle 1 tablespoon cold, sweetened espresso-style coffee over each lot of cake. Chop 125 g (4 oz) stoned prunes and divide between the dishes. Sprinkle 1 tablespoon coarsely grated dark chocolate into each one. In a separate bowl, beat together 200 g (7 oz) mascarpone and 200 g (7 oz) chilled thick custard with 2 tablespoons coffee cream liqueur (such as Kahlua). Spoon over the prunes and top each dish with a further tablespoon grated chocolate and 1 sliced prune to decorate, if desired. Chill for 10 minutes before serving.

30 ◑ Orange and Lemon Curd Cheesecakes

Serves 4

150 g (5 oz) digestive biscuits, crushed

50 g (2 oz) butter, melted and cooled

8 scant tablespoons orange curd

3 tablespoons lemon curd

250 g (8 oz) mascarpone or cream cheese

4 tablespoons double cream

2 tablespoons icing sugar, sifted

orange and lemon jelly slices or mixed fresh berries, to decorate

- Put the biscuit crumbs and butter into a bowl and mix until the texture seems damp. Spoon into 4 individual serving glasses and press down with the back of the spoon. Place 1 scant tablespoon orange curd on each biscuit base.

- Place the lemon curd in a bowl with the mascarpone, double cream and icing sugar and beat until smooth and thick. Spoon half the mixture into the glasses. Top with another scant tablespoon of orange curd followed by the remaining mascarpone. Chill for 15–20 minutes, then decorate with the jelly slices or mixed berries, as preferred.

---

1 Orange and Lemon Curd Creams

Arrange 8 broken sponge fingers in the bottom of 4 glass serving dishes and pour 1 tablespoon limoncello liqueur over each one. Allow to soak in for 5 minutes, then top each one with 1 scant tablespoon orange curd. Meanwhile, beat 3 tablespoons lemon curd and 2 tablespoons sifted icing sugar into 300 g (10 oz) fromage blanc and spoon over the sponge fingers. Crush 12 amaretti biscuits and sprinkle over the orange and lemon curd creams, to serve.

2 Orange and Lemon Curd Buttons

Put 175 g (6 oz) softened butter into a bowl with 150 g (5 oz) caster sugar, 1 large lightly beaten egg and 75 g (3 oz) ground almonds. Beat together, then add 250 g (8 oz) plain flour and mix to form a soft dough. Roll into about 24 balls, place them on 2 baking sheets lined with baking paper and flatten slightly. Make a dent in the centre of each one and fill half the biscuits with ½ teaspoon lemon curd and the remaining half with orange curd. Bake in a preheated oven, 200°C (400°F), Gas Mark 6, for about 12 minutes, or until lightly golden. Transfer to wire racks to cool.

1 Toasted Ginger Syrup Waffles

Serves 4

50 g (2 oz) butter
4 tablespoons double cream
2 tablespoons soft dark
    brown sugar
15 g (½ oz) stem ginger, drained
    and finely chopped
2 tablespoons stem ginger syrup
8 Belgian-style toasting waffles
good-quality vanilla ice cream,
    to serve

- Place the butter in a small pan with the cream, sugar, stem ginger and syrup. Warm over a low heat for 5–6 minutes, stirring occasionally, until the butter has melted and the sugar dissolved.

- Meanwhile, toast the waffles according to the packet instructions and arrange on serving plates. Top with a scoop of ice cream and serve warm, drizzled with the ginger syrup.

---

2 Ginger Syrup Pain Perdu

Prepare the ginger syrup as in the main recipe. Meanwhile, place 2 eggs in a large, shallow bowl with 100 g (3½ oz) caster sugar and 250 ml (8 fl oz) milk and whisk until smooth. Dip 4 slices of slightly stale brioche into the mixture, turning to coat both sides. Melt 75 g (3 oz) unsalted butter in a large, nonstick frying pan and cook the brioche over a medium-low heat for 4–5 minutes, turning once, until golden. Arrange on plates and top with a scoop of vanilla ice cream, a dusting of icing sugar and a drizzle of the ginger syrup.

3 Ginger Syrup Sponge Puddings

Prepare the ginger syrup as in the main recipe. Grease 4 mini pudding basins (150 ml/¼ pint capacity) and place 1 tablespoon syrup in each one. Put 75 g (3 oz) softened butter in a large bowl and beat in 75 g (3 oz) caster sugar, 75 g (3 oz) self-raising flour, 1 large egg and 1 teaspoon ground ginger. When creamy, spoon into the basins. Bake in a preheated oven, 180°C (350°F), Gas Mark 4, for 15–18 minutes, until risen, golden and firm to the touch. Allow to cool for a minute or two, then carefully invert into serving dishes. Serve with a scoop of vanilla ice cream and the remaining syrup.

3⦿ Brown Sugar Plum Turnovers

Serves 6

320 g (10¾ oz) shop-bought
   sheet of puff pastry
150 g (5 oz) shop-bought custard
1 tablespoon soft light
   brown sugar
1 teaspoon ground cinnamon
2 tablespoons ground almonds
1 teaspoon finely grated orange
   rind, plus extra to garnish
5 plums, halved, stoned and
   thinly sliced
1 small egg, beaten
demerara sugar, to sprinkle
sweetened mascarpone, to serve
   (optional)

- Line a baking sheet with baking paper.

- Unroll the pastry and cut it into 6 x 10 cm (4 inch) squares. Place on the prepared baking sheet and spread the custard over them, leaving a 1 cm (½ inch) border around the edges.

- Put the brown sugar into a bowl with the cinnamon, almonds and orange rind and mix well. Add the plums and toss to coat, then arrange a diagonal row of them across the middle of each pastry.

- Brush the border with beaten egg, then bring 2 diagonally opposite corners together and press to seal. Brush the pastries with the remaining egg and sprinkle 1 teaspoon demerara sugar over each one. Bake in a preheated oven, 200°C (400°F), Gas Mark 6, for 15–20 minutes, until the pastry is crisp and golden. Serve warm with sweetened mascarpone garnished with grated orange rind, if desired.

 ### Brown Sugar Grilled Plums

Halve and stone 8–12 plums, depending on their size, and arrange cut-side up in a shallow ovenproof dish. Drizzle over 2 tablespoons orange juice, dust with 1 teaspoon ground cinnamon and sprinkle generously with 4 tablespoons soft light brown sugar. Slide under a preheated medium-hot grill for 5–7 minutes, until the sugar is melting and golden. Allow to cool slightly and serve with sweetened mascarpone, if desired.

 ### Brown Sugar Poached Plums

Pour 400 ml (14 fl oz) cranberry juice and 200 ml (7 fl oz) water into a saucepan with 1 small cinnamon stick, 2 strips orange peel and 2 tablespoons soft light brown sugar. Stir over a medium heat to dissolve the sugar, then add 8–12 halved plums, depending on their size, and simmer for about 10 minutes, or until tender. Allow to cool slightly and serve with sweetened mascarpone, if desired.

Melting Chocolate and Date Fondants

Serves 6

125 g (4 oz) butter, plus extra to grease

75 g (3 oz) plain flour, plus extra for dusting

150 g (5 oz) dark chocolate, broken into pieces

75 g (3 oz) stoned dates, chopped

2 large eggs, plus 2 large egg yolks

75 g (3 oz) soft light brown sugar

clotted cream or ice cream, to serve

- Grease 6 mini pudding basins (150 ml/¼ pint capacity) and dust lightly with flour, tapping to remove any excess.

- Warm the butter with the chocolate and dates in a small pan over a low heat, stirring occasionally until just melted. Set aside to cool slightly.

- Meanwhile, put the eggs, egg yolks and sugar into a bowl and beat with a hand-held electric whisk for 2–3 minutes, until pale and thick. Sift the flour into the bowl and mix together, then fold in the chocolate mixture.

- Divide the batter between the prepared pudding basins. Place on a baking sheet and bake in a preheated oven, 190°C (375°F), Gas Mark 5, for about 10 minutes, until risen and just firm (the top should still be slightly yielding). Set aside to rest for 1–2 minutes, then invert into shallow serving dishes. Serve with clotted cream or ice cream.

Saucy Chocolate and Date Brownies

Arrange 6 shop-bought chocolate brownies in an ovenproof dish, overlapping them slightly. Stir 100 g (3½ oz) stoned and chopped dates into 300 g (10 oz) warmed, Belgian-style chocolate sauce and drizzle the mixture over the brownies. Place in a preheated oven, 200°C (400°F), Gas Mark 6, for 7–8 minutes, until warmed through. Serve in shallow dishes with clotted cream or ice cream.

White Chocolate Chunk and Date

Brownies Melt 175 g (6 oz) butter in a small pan with 200 g (7 oz) dark chocolate, broken into pieces, stirring occasionally until just melted. Take off the heat and stir in 100 g (3½ oz) stoned, chopped dates. Beat 3 eggs in a large bowl with 150 g (5 oz) golden caster sugar, until pale and creamy. Add the cooled chocolate mixture plus 75 g (3 oz) self-raising flour and 150 g (5 oz) white chocolate chunks. Mix gently to combine. Line a 23 cm (9 inch) square brownie tin with baking paper, allowing it to stand a little above the sides. Pour in the brownie mixture and bake in a preheated oven, 190°C (375°F), Gas Mark 5, for about 20 minutes, until just firm to the touch. Cool in the tin, then cut into squares to serve.

10 Figgy Rice Pudding Brûlée

Serves 4

8 teaspoons good-quality
fig conserve

500 g (1 lb) chilled, good-quality
rice pudding

75 g (3 oz) ready-to-eat dried
figs, chopped

1 teaspoon finely grated lemon
rind (optional)

50 g (2 oz) caster sugar

- Set out 4 small heatproof dishes or ramekins and place
2 teaspoons of fig conserve in each one.

- Empty the rice pudding into a bowl and stir in the figs, and
lemon rind, if using. Spoon into the dishes.

- Sprinkle an even layer of the caster sugar over the puddings
and caramelize it with a blowtorch or under a very hot grill
for 1–2 minutes.

- Set aside for 1–2 minutes, until the brûlée hardens, then
serve immediately.

20 Rice Pudding with Roasted Figs

Place 8 halved figs, cut-side up,
in an ovenproof dish. Place 25 g
(1 oz) butter in a small pan with
2 tablespoons clear honey and
2 teaspoons lemon juice and heat
gently until warm. Pour over
the figs and bake in a preheated
oven, 180°C (350°F), Gas Mark 4,
for 15–20 minutes, until tender.
Meanwhile, warm 500 g (1 lb)
good-quality rice pudding in a
pan over a medium-low heat,
stirring occasionally, until hot.
Spoon into dishes and serve
with the roasted figs.

30 Figgy Rice Pudding

Place 125 g (4 oz)
pudding rice in a large saucepan
with 750 ml (1¼ pints) milk, 50 g
(2 oz) soft light brown sugar,
25 g (1 oz) butter and 1 teaspoon
finely grated lemon rind
(optional). Bring to the boil over
a medium heat, stirring frequently
to prevent burning, then simmer
for about 25 minutes, adding
more milk if it seems a little
dry. Add 75 g (3 oz) chopped,
ready-to-eat dried figs for the
final 5 minutes. Spoon into bowls
and top each one with a spoonful
of fig conserve.

10 Mulled Spice Apple Juice

Serves 6

1.5 litres (2½ pints) pressed
  apple juice
4 cloves
2 star anise
1 small cinnamon stick
2.5 cm (1 inch) piece of fresh
  root ginger, peeled and sliced
1 small orange, cut into thin slices
clear honey, to taste
50–75 ml (2–3 fl oz) calvados
  or brandy (optional)

- Place all the ingredients, except the calvados, in a saucepan and bring to the boil. Simmer gently for 7–8 minutes, until aromatic, then take off the heat.

- Add the desired amount of calvados, or omit completely for a non-alcoholic version. Serve in a punch bowl, if desired, and pour into heatproof glasses.

2 Spiced Apple Pie Cupcakes

Sift 125 g (4 oz) self-raising flour into a bowl, then sift in 1 teaspoon baking powder and 1½ teaspoons ground mixed spice. Add 100 g (3½ oz) softened butter, 125 g (4 oz) soft dark brown sugar, 2 tablespoons apple purée, 1 small peeled and grated apple and 2 eggs and beat well. Line a 12-hole muffin tin with paper cases and spoon in the cake mixture. Bake in a preheated oven, 190°C (375°F), Gas Mark 5, for 12–14 minutes, until risen and firm. Meanwhile, put 150 ml (¼ pint) double cream into a bowl and beat in 150 g (5 oz) cream cheese, ½ teaspoon ground cinnamon and 2 tablespoons sifted icing sugar. Serve the cupcakes topped with a dollop of the spiced cream cheese icing.

3 Spiced Tarte aux Pommes

Unroll a 375 g (12 oz) puff pastry sheet and place on a baking sheet lined with baking paper. Brush with butter and bake in a preheated oven, 190°C (375°F), Gas Mark 5, for 8–10 minutes, until beginning to puff and turn golden. Meanwhile, peel, core and slice 4 dessert apples and cut into thin wedges. Place in a large pan with 50 g (2 oz) butter, 2 tablespoons golden caster sugar and 1 teaspoon ground mixed spice. Cook gently over a medium-low heat, turning occasionally, until tender and lightly golden. Spoon the apples evenly and attractively over the pastry, leaving a clear narrow border around the edge. Return to the oven for a further 8–10 minutes, until the pastry is crisp and golden. Set aside to cool slightly, then brush the tarte with 50 g (2 oz) melted apricot conserve. Serve with whipped cream and a dusting of ground cinnamon, if desired.

Chunky Double Choc-Chip Cookies

Serves 6–8

150 g (5 oz) softened butter
200 g (7 oz) caster sugar
1 egg, lightly beaten
200 g (7 oz) plain flour
25 g (1 oz) cocoa powder
½ teaspoon bicarbonate of soda
75 g (3 oz) white chocolate chunks
75 g (3 oz) dark chocolate chunks

- Line 2 large baking sheets with baking paper.

- Put the butter and sugar into a bowl and beat together until pale and creamy. Beat in the egg, then stir in the flour, cocoa powder, bicarbonate of soda and chocolate chunks.

- Heap 8–9 rough-textured spoonfuls of the batter on to each prepared baking sheet, spacing them well apart so they have room to spread. Bake in a preheated oven, 180°C (350°F), Gas Mark 4, for about 10 minutes, until slightly firm around the edges. Transfer to a wire rack to cool slightly before serving.

 Chocolate Chip Cookie Crumbles

Place 200 g (7 oz) shop-bought chocolate chip cookies in a freezer bag and tap with a rolling pin until crumbled but not powdery. Pour 1 tablespoon thick dark chocolate sauce into the bottom of 6 individual serving glasses. Place 400 g (13 oz) thick Greek yogurt in a bowl and gently stir through a further 4 tablespoons chocolate sauce to create a marbled effect. Spoon half the mixture into the glasses, then top with half the cookie crumble. Repeat with the remaining yogurt and cookie crumble, then serve.

 Chocolate Chip Rock Cakes

Sift 175 g (6 oz) self-raising flour, 25 g (1 oz) cocoa powder and 1 teaspoon baking powder into a large bowl. Add 100 g (3½ oz) diced butter and rub in with your fingertips until the mixture resembles breadcrumbs. Finely chop 100 g (3½ oz) shop-bought chocolate chip cookie dough and stir into the flour with 50 g (2 oz) white chocolate chips. Add 1 lightly beaten egg and 1–2 tablespoons milk, just enough to make a stiff but sticky mixture. Line 2 large baking sheets with baking paper and spoon 10–12 rough-textured mounds on to them, spacing them well apart. Bake in a preheated oven, 200°C (400°F), Gas Mark 6, for 18–20 minutes, until lightly golden. Transfer to wire racks to cool.

30 Freeform Pear and Blackberry Pie

Serves 4–6

1 tablespoon fine semolina or polenta (not the quick-cook variety)

250 g (8 oz) shop-bought shortcrust pastry

flour, for dusting

1 egg white, lightly whisked

3 ripe but firm pears, peeled, cored and cut into wedges

125 g (4 oz) frozen blackberries

2 tablespoons demerara sugar

½ teaspoon ground cinnamon

½ teaspoon ground ginger

clotted cream, to serve (optional)

- Line a baking sheet with baking paper, then sprinkle the semolina or polenta evenly over the baking sheet. Place the pastry on a lightly floured work surface and roll into a circle about 33 cm (13 inches) wide. Transfer to the prepared baking sheet and brush with the egg white.

- Pile the pears and blackberries into the centre of the pastry, leaving a 3.5 cm (1½ inch) empty border around the edge. Mix the sugar, cinnamon and ginger in a bowl and sprinkle 1½ tablespoons of this mixture over the fruit.

- Lift up the plain border and fold it over at regular intervals around the fruit, making a tuck now and then to keep the pie a roughly circular shape. The centre of the filling will still be visible. Brush with egg white and sprinkle with the remaining sugar mixture. Bake in a preheated oven, 220°C (425°F), Gas Mark 7, for 20–25 minutes, until the pastry is crisp and golden. Serve warm with clotted cream, if desired.

 Pear and Blackberry Layered Crunch Place 200 g (7 oz) crushed ginger nut biscuits in a bowl with 75 g (3 oz) melted butter and mix well. Place 1 tablespoonful blackberry conserve or jam in the bottom of 4 individual glass dishes. Put 250 g (8 oz) chilled thick custard and 150 g (5 oz) Greek yogurt into a bowl and beat together. Spoon half the mixture over the conserve, then sprinkle half the crushed biscuits on top. Drain and slice a 400 g (13 oz) can pear halves and arrange over the biscuits. Layer the remaining custard and biscuits as before, then serve, decorated with a few blackberries, if desired.

 Pear and Blackberry Fruit Gratin Place the pears, blackberries and spices from the main recipe in a large bowl, add 2 tablespoons soft light brown sugar and mix well. Transfer to an ovenproof dish and slide under a preheated medium-hot grill for 4–5 minutes. Meanwhile, combine 300 g (10 oz) thick vanilla custard with 200 g (7 oz) Greek yogurt. Pour it over the grilled fruit and sprinkle with 3 tablespoons demerara sugar. Slide the dish back under the grill for 3–4 minutes, until the sugar is melting and beginning to caramelize.

Cinnamon-Spiked Raisin Scones

Serves 4–5

325 g (11 oz) self-raising flour, plus extra for dusting
1 teaspoon baking powder
1 teaspoon ground cinnamon
pinch of salt
75 g (3 oz) butter, diced
50 g (2 oz) dark soft brown sugar
75 g (3 oz) golden raisins
175 ml (6 fl oz) buttermilk
1 small egg, lightly beaten
clotted cream, to serve

- Sift the flour, baking powder, cinnamon and salt into a large bowl. Add the butter and rub in with your fingertips, until the mixture resembles fine breadcrumbs. Stir in the sugar and raisins. Pour the buttermilk into the dry ingredients, mixing to form a soft but not sticky dough.

- Place on a lightly floured work surface and roll out to a thickness of about 2.5 cm (1 inch). Using a 5 cm (2 inch) cutter, stamp out 10–12 circles.

- Arrange the scones on a large baking sheet, brush the tops with the beaten egg and bake in a preheated oven, 220°C (425°F), Gas Mark 7, for 10–15 minutes, until risen and golden. Transfer to wire racks to cool, and serve warm or cold with clotted cream.

 Cinnamon and Raisin Drop Scones

Sift 200 g (7 oz) self-raising flour into a large bowl followed by 1 teaspoon baking powder and 1 teaspoon cinnamon. Stir in 3 tablespoons dark soft brown sugar, then make a well in the centre. Break 1 large egg into a jug and whisk in 250 ml (8 fl oz) of buttermilk. Pour into the well and whisk together until the mixture is smooth and thick. Stir in 50 g (2 oz) golden raisins. Brush a large, nonstick frying pan with a little melted butter and place over a medium heat. Add tablespoons of the scone mixture to the pan, give them a little space to expand, and cook for about 1 minute on each side, flipping them over once bubbles begin to appear on the surface. Cook for a further 30 seconds, until golden, then stack up on warmed serving plates and serve with clotted cream and dusted with a little extra cinnamon, if desired.

30 **Cinnamon Raisin Sponge Traybake**

Place 125 g (4 oz) softened butter in a bowl and add 100 g (3½ oz) golden caster sugar, 125 g (4 oz) sifted self-raising flour, 1 teaspoon baking powder, 1 teaspoon ground cinnamon, 2 large eggs and 2 tablespoons golden syrup. Beat with an electric whisk until creamy, then fold in 75 g (3 oz) golden raisins. Line a 23 cm (9 inch) square cake tin with baking paper, allowing it to stand above the edges, and fill with the sponge mixture. Bake in a preheated oven, 190°C (375°F), Gas Mark 5, for 20 minutes, until risen and firm. Carefully lift on to a wire rack to cool slightly, then cut into squares to serve.

30 Mandarin and Vanilla Seed Brownies

Serves 6–8

175 (6 oz) butter

200 g (7 oz) plain or orange-flavoured dark chocolate, broken into pieces

3 large eggs

seeds from 1 vanilla pod

75 g (3 oz) dark soft brown sugar

100 g (3½ oz) caster sugar

75 g (3 oz) self-raising flour

298 g (10 oz) can mandarin segments in juice, drained

- Line a 23 cm (9 inch) square cake tin with baking paper, allowing it to stand a bit above the edges.

- Warm the butter and chocolate in a small pan over a low heat, stirring occasionally, until just melted. Set aside.

- Meanwhile, put the eggs, vanilla seeds and sugars into a large bowl and beat until thick and pale. Sift in the flour, mix well, then stir in the melted chocolate.

- Fill the prepared tin with the brownie mixture and sprinkle the mandarin segments over the top.

- Bake in a preheated oven, 190°C (375°F), Gas Mark 5, for about 20 minutes, or until just firm to the touch but with a slightly fudgy texture. Cool slightly in the tin, then lift on to a board and cut into squares to serve.

 Mandarin and Vanilla Brûlée

Drain 2 x 298 g (10 oz) cans mandarin segments and divide between 6 individual heatproof dishes. Place 300 g (10 oz) crème fraîche in a bowl with 2 teaspoons vanilla bean paste, 3 tablespoons sifted icing sugar and 1 tablespoon orange liqueur, such as Grand Marnier or Cointreau. Beat together, then spoon the mixture over the mandarins. Sprinkle 2 teaspoons caster sugar on top of each pudding and caramelize with a blowtorch or under a very hot grill for 1–2 minutes. Serve as soon as the golden brûlée has hardened.

 Homemade Vanilla Custard with Mandarins Place 4 large egg yolks in a bowl with 1 teaspoon vanilla bean paste and 100 g (3½ oz) sugar and whisk together. Bring 350 ml (12 fl oz) milk to the boil, then pour into the eggs in a steady stream, whisking constantly. Pour into a clean pan and place over a very low heat, whisking constantly until the custard thickens and taking care it does not boil. Take off the heat, stir 150 ml (¼ pint) double cream into the custard and serve immediately with 2 x 298 g (10 oz) cans drained mandarin segments.

10 Cinnamon-Spiced Banana Flambé

Serves 6

75 g (3 oz) butter
6 ripe but firm bananas, peeled
50 g (2 oz) dark soft brown sugar
1 teaspoon ground cinnamon
6 tablespoons dark or spiced rum
rum raisin ice cream, to serve
50 g (2 oz) pecan halves,
  lightly crushed

- Melt the butter in a wide pan over a medium heat. Slice the bananas in half lengthways, add to the pan and cook for 3–4 minutes, carefully turning once, until golden on both sides. Sprinkle over the sugar and cinnamon and heat gently to dissolve.

- Pour in the rum and carefully ignite it with a long match to flambé the bananas. Allow the flames to die out while spooning the liquid over the fruit.

- Arrange the bananas on warmed serving plates with a scoop of ice cream, then sprinkle with the pecans and serve immediately.

20 Cinnamon-Spiced Banoffee Pecan

Pie Place 125 g (4 oz) pecan halves in a heavy-based frying pan and toast over a medium-low heat for 2–3 minutes, shaking the pan frequently. Add 50 g (2 oz) caster sugar and 1 teaspoon ground cinnamon and stir occasionally, until the sugar melts. Simmer, without stirring, until the sugar turns golden brown. Pour the mixture on to a greaseproof paper-lined baking sheet and set aside somewhere cool (not the refrigerator) to harden. Meanwhile, spread 260 g (8½ oz) thick salted caramel sauce or dulce de leche over a 25 cm (10 inch) sponge flan base. Top with 4 sliced bananas. Whip 200 ml (7 fl oz) double cream with ½ teaspoon ground cinnamon and 2 tablespoons sifted icing sugar until soft peaks form, then spoon over the bananas. Break up the caramelized pecans with a rolling pin and scatter over the pie to serve.

30 Spiced Banana and Pecan Pie

Lightly grease a loose-bottomed, 23 cm (9 inch) fluted tart tin and line with a 320 g (10¾ oz) sheet of shop-bought shortcrust pastry, trimming off the excess. Put 2 large eggs into a bowl, add 1 teaspoon ground cinnamon, 50 g (2 oz) caster sugar, 150 g (5 oz) golden syrup, 25 g (1 oz) melted butter and 1 tablespoon lemon juice and beat to combine. Cover the bottom of the pastry case with 1 sliced banana and 150 g (5 oz) pecan halves. Pour over the batter and bake in a preheated oven, 220°C (425°F), Gas Mark 7, for 18–20 minutes. Cool slightly in the tin, then transfer to a plate, cut into slices and serve warm with a scoop of ice cream, as above.

3⊙ Rhubarb and Clementine Crumbles

Serves 4

539 g (1 lb 1½ oz) can rhubarb
  in light syrup, drained
100 g (3½ oz) frozen raspberries
125 ml (4 fl oz) freshly squeezed
  clementine juice
15 g (½ oz) stem ginger, drained
  and finely chopped
125 g (4 oz) plain flour
75 g (3 oz) butter
100 g (3½ oz) soft light
  brown sugar
3 tablespoons porridge oats
2 tablespoons toasted flaked
  almonds
pinch of salt
raspberry ripple ice cream,
  to serve

- Combine the rhubarb and raspberries in a bowl with the clementine juice and ginger. Divide between 4 shallow, individual ovenproof dishes.

- Put the flour into a bowl and rub in the butter until the mixture resembles breadcrumbs. Stir in the sugar, oats, almonds and salt, then sprinkle this mixture over the rhubarb.

- Bake in a preheated oven, 190°C (375°F), Gas Mark 5, for about 18–20 minutes, until the topping is crisp and golden. Serve with a scoop of raspberry ripple ice cream.

 Rhubarb and Clementine Crumble Fool Crush 100 g (3½ oz) defrosted raspberries and spoon into 4 glass serving dishes. Place 500 g (1 lb) Greek yogurt in a bowl with a drained 539 g (1 lb 1½ oz) can rhubarb, 2 tablespoons clementine juice, 15 g (½ oz) finely chopped stem ginger and 1–2 tablespoons soft light brown sugar, depending on sweetness desired. Fold together, then spoon over the raspberries. Top each dish with a small handful of crunchy oat and nut cereal and serve immediately.

 Roasted Rhubarb with Clementines Cut 500 g (1 lb) rhubarb into 3.5 cm (1½ inch) lengths and place in a large ovenproof dish. Slice the peel and membrane away from 2 clementines, then cut into 1 cm (½ inch) slices and add to the rhubarb. Sprinkle with 3–4 tablespoons soft light brown sugar, depending on sweetness desired, then add the raspberries and stem ginger from the main recipe. Roast in a preheated oven, 200°C (400°F), Gas Mark 6, for about 15 minutes, stirring once or twice, until tender. Remove from the oven and cool slightly before serving with scoops of raspberry ripple ice cream.

Vanilla Cupcakes with Warm Blackberry Coulis

Serves 6

125 g (4 oz) butter, softened, plus extra for greasing

200 g (7 oz) frozen or fresh blackberries

2 tablespoons freshly squeezed orange juice

175 g (6 oz) caster sugar

2 teaspoons vanilla bean paste

75 g (3 oz) self-raising flour

50 g (2 oz) ground almonds

2 eggs

2 tablespoons double cream

- Grease a 12-hole muffin tin.

- Place the blackberries in a pan with the orange juice, 50 g (2 oz) of the caster sugar and 1 teaspoon of the vanilla bean paste. Place over a medium-low heat, stirring occasionally, until the sugar dissolves and the fruit collapses.

- Meanwhile, beat all the remaining ingredients together until creamy. Spoon the mixture into the prepared tin and bake in a preheated oven, 190°C (375°F), Gas Mark 5, for 12–15 minutes, until risen and firm.

- Pour the warm blackberry mixture into a blender or food processor and whizz until smooth. Pour into a jug.

- Serve the cupcakes warm with the warm blackberry coulis.

Blackberry and Vanilla Baskets

Whisk 150 ml (¼ pint) double cream with 1 tablespoon sifted icing sugar and 1 teaspoon vanilla bean paste until soft peaks form. Fold in 150 g (5 oz) shop-bought custard. Place 150 g (5 oz) blackberries in a blender or food processor with 2 tablespoons icing sugar and 1 teaspoon vanilla bean paste and whizz until smooth. Spoon the vanilla cream into 6 brandysnap baskets and serve immediately, drizzled with the coulis.

Blackberry and Vanilla Tart

Roll out 200 g (7 oz) shop-bought sweet shortcrust pastry and use to line a lightly greased 23 cm (9 inch) fluted tart tin, trimming off the excess. Chill for a few minutes. Meanwhile, beat 100 g (3½ oz) softened butter with 75 g (3 oz) ground almonds, 75 g (3 oz) caster sugar, 2 eggs, 1 teaspoon vanilla bean paste, 50 g (2 oz) self-raising flour and 2 tablespoons double cream. Spoon evenly into the chilled pastry case and scatter 125 g (4 oz) blackberries over the top. Bake in a preheated oven, 200°C (400°F), Gas Mark 6, for about 22 minutes, until golden and firm to the touch. Serve drizzled with the blackberry coulis from the main recipe.

10 Caramelized Apple and Hazelnut Filos

Serves 4–6

125 g (4 oz) unsalted butter
5 dessert apples, peeled, cored and sliced into thin wedges
2 tablespoons dark soft brown sugar
1½ teaspoons lemon juice
3 sheets of filo pastry, about 30 x 40 cm (12 x 16 inches)
2 tablespoons roasted chopped hazelnuts
warmed toffee sauce, to drizzle (optional)

- Melt the butter in a large frying pan and pour one-third of it into a small dish. Add the apples, sugar and lemon juice to the pan and cook over a medium heat for 7–8 minutes, turning occasionally, until tender and golden. Set aside.

- Meanwhile, brush each filo sheet with the reserved melted butter and lay the 3 sheets on top of one another. Cut the stacked sheets into 12 squares, then use these to line a 12-hole bun tray, arranging them at slightly different angles. Bake in a preheated oven, 220°C (425°F), Gas Mark 7, for 7–8 minutes, until crisp and golden.

- Arrange the filo pastry cases on serving plates and fill with the caramelized apples and roasted hazelnuts. Serve with warm toffee sauce, if desired.

 American Apple and Hazelnut Pancakes Sift 200 g (7 oz) plain flour, 1 teaspoon ground cinnamon (optional) and 2 teaspoons baking powder into a large bowl and make a well in the centre. Break 2 eggs into a separate bowl, add 125 ml (4 fl oz) milk and 3 tablespoons caster sugar and whisk together. Pour into the well and whisk again, slowly incorporating the flour from the sides. Stir in 2 tablespoons chopped roasted hazelnuts and 1 small peeled, cored and coarsely grated apple. Melt a small knob of butter in a large, nonstick frying pan and pour in 4 or 5 small ladlefuls of the batter to form small thick pancakes. Cook over a medium-low heat for 2–3 minutes, until bubbles start to appear on the surface. Flip over and cook for a further 30–60 seconds, until golden. Repeat with the remaining batter to make about 18 pancakes. Serve warm, drizzled with maple syrup, if desired.

Apple and Hazelnut Strudels Drain a 385 g (12½ oz) can apple slices and place in a bowl with 1 teaspoon ground cinnamon, 2 tablespoons roasted chopped hazelnuts, 2 tablespoons soft dark brown sugar and 1 teaspoon grated lemon rind. Mix. Butter and stack 3 filo pastry sheets as above. Cut each stack into 3 rectangles. Sprinkle each rectangle with 2 teaspoons ground hazelnuts, then spoon over the filling. Roll up, tucking in the edges. Bake the strudels on a lined baking sheet in a preheated oven, 220°C (425°F), Gas Mark 7, for 15–20 minutes, or until crisp and golden. Serve drizzled with warm toffee sauce.

30 Canned Cherry and Apricot Cobbler

Serves 6

2 x 425 g (14 oz) cans stoneless
  cherries in syrup
410 g (13½ oz) can apricot halves
  in juice, drained
2 tablespoons Amaretto liqueur
  or 2 tablespoons canned
  apricot juice
100 g (3½ oz) plain flour
1 teaspoon mixed spice (optional)
50 g (2 oz) butter, diced
25 g (1 oz) demerara sugar
pinch of salt
1 egg, lightly beaten
25 g (1 oz) rolled oats
ice cream or custard, to serve
  (optional)

- Empty 1 can of cherries into a saucepan with the apricots and Amaretto or juice. Drain the second can of cherries and add the fruit to the pan. Place over a medium-low heat for 3–4 minutes, until warm.

- Sift the flour and mixed spice (if using) into a bowl and rub in the butter with your fingertips until the mixture resembles breadcrumbs. Stir in the sugar and salt, then add the egg and mix briefly to form a dough.

- Pour the fruit mixture into a large ovenproof dish. Arrange small mounds of the dough over the top, then sprinkle with the oats. Bake in a preheated oven, 200°C (400°F), Gas Mark 6, for 18–20 minutes, until bubbling and golden.

- Spoon the cobbler into dishes and serve with ice cream or custard, if desired.

10 Canned Cherries and Crunchy Oats

Put 75 g (3 oz) rolled oats in a bowl and mix with 50 g (2 oz) soft dark brown sugar, 50 g (2 oz) melted butter and 50 g (2 oz) chopped nuts. Tip into a large, nonstick frying pan and toast gently over a medium low-heat for 6–7 minutes, stirring frequently, until crisp and golden. Transfer to a plate and set aside. Meanwhile, warm the canned fruit with the Amaretto as in the main recipe. Spoon into dishes and serve topped with the crunchy oats.

20 Canned Cherry Crumble

Warm the canned fruit as in the main recipe. Meanwhile, combine the oats, sugar, melted butter and chopped nuts from the 10-minute recipe, without toasting. Tip the fruit into an ovenproof dish and cover with the crumble topping. Bake in a preheated oven, 200°C (400°F), Gas Mark 6, for about 15 minutes, or until the topping is crisp and golden. Serve with ice cream or custard, as above.

10 Whipped Irish Cream Hot Chocolate

Serves 4

200 g (7 oz) coarsely grated dark chocolate, plus extra for sprinkling
900 ml (1½ pints) milk
150 ml (¼ pint) double cream
1 tablespoon icing sugar
75 ml (3 fl oz) Irish cream liqueur
1–2 tablespoons caster sugar, according to taste

- Place the chocolate in a large heatproof jug. Heat the milk in a pan until it is almost simmering.

- Meanwhile, whip the double cream with the icing sugar until it forms soft peaks, then fold in 1 tablespoon of the cream liqueur.

- Pour about a quarter of the hot milk into the jug, stirring until the chocolate has melted. Add the remaining milk in a steady stream, stirring constantly. Add the remaining Irish cream and sweeten to taste with the caster sugar.

- Pour the hot chocolate into mugs and top with the desired quantity of whipped cream. Sprinkle with a little extra grated chocolate to decorate, and serve immediately.

20 Spiced Irish Cream Latté

Heat 600 ml (1 pint) milk in a pan with 1 small cinnamon stick, ¼ teaspoon ground nutmeg and 2–3 blades of mace. Heat until almost boiling, then take off the heat and stir in 75 ml (3 fl oz) Irish cream liqueur. Keep warm for about 10 minutes to allow the flavours to develop. Meanwhile, prepare 4 strong, espresso-style coffees in large mugs. Strain the spiced milk over the espressos and serve immediately, sweetened with sugar or honey, if desired.

30 Irish Cream Cup of Chai

Place 3 tablespoons loose black tea leaves in a large pan with 1 cinnamon stick, 4 cloves, 1 star anise, 3 crushed cardamom pods, 4 coriander seeds and a 1.5 cm (¾ inch) piece of peeled and sliced fresh root ginger. Pour in 750 ml (1¼ pints) milk and place over a low heat for about 20 minutes, stirring occasionally, without boiling. Take the chai off the heat and stir in 75 ml (3 fl oz) Irish cream liqueur. Strain into warmed mugs and sweeten to taste with clear honey.

30 Fire and Ice Winter Berry Meringue Pie

Serves 6

400 g (13 oz) frozen fruits
250 g (8 oz) mascarpone
1 teaspoon vanilla bean paste
2 tablespoons icing sugar
3 tablespoons crème de cassis
  or cranberry juice
1 x 25 cm (10 inch) sponge
  flan base
3 large egg whites
150 g (5 oz) caster sugar
redcurrants or other berries,
  to decorate (optional)

- Line a baking sheet with baking paper.

- Place the frozen fruits in a bowl or food processor with the mascarpone, vanilla paste, icing sugar and crème de cassis or cranberry juice. Beat or pulse until very thick and smooth.

- Spread the fruit mixture over the sponge base in a thick, even layer. Place on the prepared baking sheet, then cover loosely with clingfilm and chill in the freezer for about 15 minutes.

- Meanwhile, make the meringue mixture by whisking the egg whites until they form soft peaks. Gradually add the caster sugar, a spoonful at a time, whisking well between each addition, until the meringue is thick, glossy and forms stiff peaks.

- Spoon the meringue mixture over the flan, using the back of the spoon to create peaks. Slide under a preheated hot grill for 1–2 minutes, until the top is beginning to colour nicely.

- Cut into wedges, decorate with redcurrants or other berries, if desired, and serve immediately.

 Icy Winter Berry Pavlovas

Place 6 individual meringue nests on serving plates. Prepare the iced berry mascarpone as in the main recipe and spoon into the meringue nests. Top each one with a dollop of whipped cream and some redcurrants. Serve immediately.

 Icy Winter Berry Meringue Trifle

Cut 1 cherry Madeira loaf cake into 2.5 cm (1 inch) cubes and arrange in the bottom of a large glass serving dish. Drizzle over 4 tablespoons crème de cassis or good-quality blackcurrant cordial and set aside to soak in. Meanwhile, prepare the iced berry mascarpone following the main recipe. In a separate bowl, whip 200 ml (7 fl oz) double cream with 1 teaspoon vanilla bean paste and 2 tablespoons sifted icing sugar, until soft peaks form. Spoon the berry mixture over the soaked sponge and cover with the whipped cream. Top with 16 mini meringues and a handful of redcurrants or other berries, and serve immediately.

20 Sticky Citrus Friands

Serves 6

175 g (6 oz) unsalted butter, melted, plus extra for greasing

5 large egg whites

1 teaspoon finely grated lemon rind

1 teaspoon finely grated lime rind

2 tablespoons thin-cut orange marmalade

75 g (3 oz) plain flour

200 g (7 oz) icing sugar

125 g (4 oz) ground almonds

pinch of salt

25 g (1 oz) caster sugar

75 ml (3 fl oz) freshly squeezed orange juice

- Brush 1 x 12-hole or 2 x 6-hole friand or cupcake tin(s) with melted butter.

- Whisk the egg whites with the citrus rinds and marmalade, until foamy but without peaks. Sift in the flour and icing sugar, add the ground almonds, melted butter and salt and gently fold together.

- Spoon the batter into the prepared tin and bake in a preheated oven, 200°C (400°F), Gas Mark 6, for about 12 minutes, until pale golden and firm to the touch.

- Meanwhile, place the caster sugar and orange juice in a small pan over a low heat and stir to dissolve. Simmer, stirring occasionally, until the juice becomes slightly syrupy, then set aside.

- Drizzle the syrup over the friands straight from the oven and leave to cool in the tin until the syrup has been absorbed.

 Sticky Citrus Sponge

Place 4 tablespoons marmalade in a small pan, add 1 tablespoon caster sugar, 3 tablespoons freshly squeezed citrus juice (1 from a lemon, 1 from a lime and 1 from an orange). Warm gently until the sugar has dissolved and the mixture is syrupy. Meanwhile, place 6 warmed lemon muffins in serving dishes. Drizzle the syrup over them and serve with a scoop of lemon or lime sorbet.

Sticky Citrus Puddings

Grease a 6-hole nonstick giant muffin tin or Yorkshire pudding tin and place 1 tablespoon fine-cut marmalade in each hole. Put 100 g (3½ oz) caster sugar into a large bowl with 100 g (3½ oz) plain flour, 75 g (3 oz) ground almonds, 1 teaspoon baking powder and ½ teaspoon bicarbonate of soda. Place 100 g (3½ oz) cooled, melted butter in a separate bowl with 125 g (4 oz) natural yogurt, 2 eggs, 1 teaspoon finely grated lemon and 1 teaspoon lime rind. Beat well, then pour into the dry ingredients and mix gently until just combined. Spoon the mixture over the marmalade and bake in a preheated oven, 190°C (375°F), Gas Mark 5, for 18–20 minutes, until risen and firm to the touch. Carefully invert the tin of puddings on to a large plate or board, then transfer each one to a serving plate. Serve with a scoop of citrus sorbet, if desired.

3⓪ Self-Saucing Chocolate Pear Pudding

Serves 6

75 g (3 oz) butter, melted and cooled, plus extra for greasing

2 x 415 g (13¼ oz) cans pear halves in juice, drained

100 ml (3½ fl oz) milk

1 large egg

125 g (4 oz) self-raising flour

3 tablespoons cocoa powder

125 g (4 oz) caster sugar

75 ml (3 fl oz) boiling water

rich vanilla ice cream, to serve (optional)

- Lightly grease a large ovenproof dish and arrange the pear halves in the bottom.

- Put the butter, milk and egg in a large bowl and beat together. Sift in the flour and 2 tablespoons of the cocoa powder, add 75 g (3 oz) of the caster sugar and beat until smooth.

- Pour the batter over the pears and smooth with the back of a spatula.

- In a separate bowl, combine the remaining caster sugar and cocoa powder with the boiling water and stir until smooth. Pour this mixture over the batter and bake in a preheated oven, 200°C (400°F), Gas Mark 6, for about 20 minutes, or until risen and firm to the touch. Set aside to rest for 1–2 minutes before serving with scoops of vanilla ice cream, if desired.

 ### 1⓪ Chocolate Pear Crumble

Drain the pears from the main recipe, and roughly dice the pears. Divide between 6 individual dishes and drizzle over 300 g (10 oz) of warmed, Belgian-style chocolate sauce. Top with 150 g (5 oz) of crushed, sweet oat biscuits and serve immediately with a scoop of vanilla ice-cream.

 ### 2⓪ Poached Pears with Chocolate

Sauce Pour 1.2 litres (1¾ pints) apple juice into a large pan with 2 tablespoons clear honey, 1 teaspoon vanilla bean paste and 2 teaspoons lemon juice. Place over a medium-high heat until almost boiling, then add 6 peeled, cored and quartered pears. Simmer for about 15 minutes, until tender. Spoon into bowls with the juice and serve drizzled with 300 g (10 oz) warmed, Belgian-style chocolate sauce and a scoop of vanilla ice cream.

30 Cinnamon Sugar Muffins

Serves 6

200 g (7 oz) plain flour
2 teaspoons baking powder
1½ teaspoons ground cinnamon
50 g (2 oz) bran
100 g (3½ oz) caster sugar
3 tablespoons demerara sugar
2 large eggs
1 ripe banana, mashed
50 g (2 oz) butter, melted
175 ml (6 fl oz) buttermilk

- Line a 12-hole muffin tin with paper cases.

- Sift the flour, baking powder and ½ teaspoon of the cinnamon into a large bowl. Stir in the bran and caster sugar. In a separate bowl, combine the remaining cinnamon with the demerara sugar.

- Put the eggs, banana, butter and buttermilk in a jug or bowl and beat well. Pour over the dry ingredients and mix until barely combined.

- Spoon the batter into the prepared tin and sprinkle with the cinnamon sugar. Bake in a preheated oven, 180°C (350°F), Gas Mark 4, for 18–20 minutes, until risen and firm to the touch.

- Transfer the muffins to wire racks and serve warm.

---

10 Cinnamon Syrup Pancakes

Gently warm 6 tablespoons maple syrup in a small pan with 1 teaspoon ground cinnamon and 1 teaspoon lemon juice. Toast 18 American-style pancakes according to the packet instructions, then arrange on 6 plates in stacks of 3. Top each stack with a small sliced banana and a small handful of blueberries. Drizzle over the cinnamon syrup and serve with a scoop of vanilla ice cream, if desired.

20 Cinnamon Sugar Cupcakes

Place 125 g (4 oz) caster sugar in a large bowl, add 125 g (4 oz) softened unsalted butter and 125 g (4 oz) self-raising flour, 1 teaspoon baking powder, 1 teaspoon ground cinnamon and 2 large eggs. Beat until pale and creamy. Line a 12-hole muffin tin with paper cases and spoon the batter into them. Bake in a preheated oven, 200°C (400°F), Gas Mark 6, for 10–14 minutes, until risen and firm to the touch. Meanwhile, combine 1 tablespoon icing sugar with ½ teaspoon ground cinnamon. Transfer the baked cupcakes to a wire rack and sift the cinnamon sugar over them to serve.

Index

Page references in *italics*
indicate photographs

Acknowledgements

Recipes by Jo McAuley
Executive Editor Eleanor Maxfield
Senior Editor Leanne Bryan
Copy Editor Trish Burgess
Art Direction Tracy Killick for Tracy Killick Art Direction and Design
Original design concept www.gradedesign.com
Designer Tracy Killick for Tracy Killick Art Direction and Design
Photographer Will Heap
Home Economist Denise Smart
Prop Stylist Liz Hippisley
Production Manager Allison Gonsalves